Elisabeth Woodbridge Morris

Studies in Jonson's Comedy

Elisabeth Woodbridge Morris

Studies in Jonson's Comedy

ISBN/EAN: 9783744795081

Printed in Europe, USA, Canada, Australia, Japan

Cover: Foto ©Thomas Meinert / pixelio.de

More available books at **www.hansebooks.com**

YALE STUDIES IN ENGLISH

ALBERT S. COOK, Editor

V

STUDIES

IN

JONSON'S COMEDY

BY
ELISABETH WOODBRIDGE, Ph. D.

LAMSON, WOLFFE AND COMPANY
BOSTON, NEW YORK, AND LONDON
1898

CONTENTS.

		PAGE
I.	Jonson's Theory of Literary Art,	5
II.	The Comedian's Material and His Attitude,	21
III.	Character Treatment in Jonson's Typical Comedy,	28
IV.	Structural Features of Jonson's Typical Comedy,	40
	1. General Structure of the Satiro-comic Plot,	40
	2. Structural Features of *Every Man in His Humour*,	46
	3. Structural Features of *Every Man out of His Humour*,	55
	4. Structural Features of *The Alchemist*,	60
	5. Structural Features of *Volpone*,	64
V.	Jonson's Romantic Comedy,	73

Appendix. Brief Discussion of the Comedies not Already Treated: 81

Cynthia's Revels. The Poetaster. Epicoene. Bartholomew Fair. The Devil Is an Ass. The Staple of News. The Magnetic Lady. The New Inn. The Case Is Altered. A Tale of a Tub.

Bibliography, ... 99
Index, ... 102

CHAPTER I.

Jonson's Theory of Literary Art.

The revival of antiquity, with the close study it involved of Latin and Greek models, led in England as elsewhere to a new sense of the dignity of letters, and a new perception of the principles underlying literature. But in England this more selfconscious and deliberate phase of the renaissance spirit was at first expressed fitfully or not at all by the great creative writers themselves. Puttenham's treatise,[1] narrowly scholastic as it was, made a beginning, but Puttenham himself was a pure theorist and rhetorician. Sidney's *Defense* with its quaint union of humorous good sense and an almost boyish fervor, gives us "The poetry rather than the art or the theory of criticism."[2] Spenser's treatise is lost to us, and we have only his correspondence with Harvey,[3] dealing, in rather a narrow spirit, with the minor question of rime and metre; Marlowe and Shakespeare had the authority but not the peculiar mental qualities needed for the formation of a corpus of poetic theory. It was with the Jacobean era that a writer came to the front who, by virtue of a singularly consistent and logical cast of mind, informed by genius only less than the greatest, and backed by an authority even greater, with his own time, than Shakespeare's, worked out a set of principles which, if they cannot be called a system, have all the inner consistency of a system, with much of its rigidity.

Moreover, Jonson's theory, conscious and deliberate though it was, was not therefore external or only par-

---

[1] Puttenham: *The Art of English Poesie*.
[2] Wylie: *Evolution of English Criticism*, p. 12.
[3] Haslewood: *The Arte of English Poesie*.

tially representative of him. It is in this respect more satisfying, though more narrow, than the theory of his great successor, Dryden, whose practice was often so sadly and bewilderingly at variance with his precepts. For Jonson was always honest and serious, and therefore consistent, and his work, squaring essentially with his principles, serves to illustrate, not to confound them.

With any other type of mind the fact that we get our knowledge of his theory largely from a note-book whose entries are all undated would be most unfortunate. In Jonson's case this is comparatively unimportant, for his was a nature that hardened young. He did, indeed, pass through a "romantic" period, but once he had reached his characteristic standpoint—from the date, that is, of *Every Man Out of His Humour*—he is stationary. From that time to the culmination of his art in *Volpone* (or, as some will have it, in *The Alchemist*), his power grows, but his attitude is unchanged; while in the last twenty years of his life, marked as they were by unpopularity and failure both social and professional, he clings with dogged tenacity to his time-worn maxims, flinging them in the teeth of his public sometimes with arrogant defiance, sometimes with an affectation of philosophical indifference that deceives no one. But, except for this sharper note of bitterness, the critical utterances of his latest prologues and epilogues and those of his earliest might have been written on the same day—in "these forty years" he has not moved an inch, and Donne's words of his writings:—"Nascuntur senes"[1] might almost as truly be applied to their author.

Perhaps no writer has ever had a more exalted conception of what poetry is and what the poet should be. Never were two spirits more unlike than Jonson and Sidney, yet, in reading *Timber*, and often in the plays themselves, one is reminded of the *Defense*, whose argu-

---
[1] Commendatory verses; Works, I, ccxliv.

ment is not unworthily summed up in the two lines, given to the younger Ovid:

"O Sacred Poesy, thou spirit of arts,
The Soul of Science, and the queen of souls."[1]

And Sidney's spirit speaks in the words:

"And the high raptures of a happy muse,
Born on the wings of her immortal thought,
That kicks at earth with a disdainful heel,
And beats at heaven's gates with her bright hoofs."[2]

He is at one with Sidney, too, in his consistent emphasis of the moral end of poetry:—

"The study of it, if we will trust Aristotle, offers to mankind a certain rule and pattern of living well and happily . . . . insomuch as the wisest and best learned have thought her the absolute mistress of manners, and nearest of kin to virtue. And whereas they entitle philosophy to be a rigid and austere poetry, they have, on the contrary, styled poesy a dulcet and gentle philosophy, which leads on and guides us by the hand to action with a ravishing delight and incredible sweetness."[3]

Indeed when he wrote that he must surely have had Sidney in mind, as one of the "wisest and best learned," so exactly do his words summarize one whole section of the *Defense*.[4] For the poet, Jonson's ideal is correspondingly high, and he reminds us of Milton as he urges that the practice of poesy "should not be attempted with unclean hands"[5]—as he asserts "the impossibility of any man's being the good poet without first being a good man."[6] But if in his emphasis of a strenuous morality Jonson was akin to the Puritanism whose follies he ridiculed, he was in temper closer to the Puritan poet of the later than to him of the earlier age. For Sidney's morality was tinged with a mysticism and soft-

---

[1] The *Poetaster;* Works, II, 386.
[2] Ib.
[3] *Timber;* Ed. Schelling, p. 74.
[4] Cf. Sidney: *Defense of Poesy*, Ed. Cook, pp. 11-32.
[5] *Volpone:* Dedicatory Letter; Works, III, 156.
[6] Ib. Cf. Longinus: *On the Sublime*, cap. IX. But cf. also, infra, pp. 19, 20.

ened by a rare and lovely humility that neither Jonson nor Milton knew.

This conviction of Jonson's that the ends of poetry are moral—that the poet is, in a strict though high sense, a teacher—can scarcely be over-emphasized, for though it did not dominate all his work,[1] it did dominate all his theorizing. It is one of the fundamental points of divergence between his drama and Shakespeare's, it marks his kinship with Juvenal and with Aristophanes, as well as the far closer kinship with Molière. But as its importance is greatest in determining the type of comedy he was to create, it can best be taken up in that connection.

Aside from a lofty morality, then, there go to the poet's making two things, natural endowment and good training. Neither avails alone, and if Jonson may seem to have laid greater emphasis on the second, this is only seeming—the natural result, perhaps, of reaction from current opinion in which the importance of natural gifts had been so over-emphasized as to make some protest inevitable.

Jonson's protest is vigorous enough. The poet is born, he admits, but he is also made, he must undergo training, " and not think he can leap forth suddenly a poet by dreaming he hath been in Parnassus, or having washed his lips, as they say, in Helicon. There goes more to his making than so."[2] But often the note of personal bitterness is discernible, as here:

" But the wretcheder are the obstinate contemners of all helps and arts; such as presuming on their own naturals, which, perhaps, are excellent, dare deride all diligence, ... and they utter all they can think with a kind of violence and indisposition, unexamined, without relation either to person, place, or any fitness else; and the more wilful and stubborn they are in it the more learned they are esteemed of the multitude, through their excellent vice of judgment, who think those things the stronger that have no art."[3]

---

[1] Cf. infra, pp. 28-31.
[2] *Timber*, Ed. Schelling, p. 77.
[3] Ib., p. 26.

That last clause is very keen, and cuts as deep to-day as when it was written. He goes on:

"It cannot but come to pass that these men who commonly seek to do more than enough may sometimes happen on something that is good and great; but very seldom: and when it comes it doth not recompence the rest of their ill."[1]

Yet, it must be remembered he never departs from his fundamental belief that "art" is powerless without "nature"—"For, as Simylus saith in Stobaeus, . . . without art nature can never be perfect; and without nature art can claim no being."[2] Once he goes even farther, admitting that both painter and poet "are born artificers, not made. Nature is more powerful in them than study."[3]

Such a position seems inexpugnable, and one is inclined to wonder at the unfairness of the critics who have set down Jonson as an advocate of a mechanical art, to be followed by rule of thumb. But the critics are partly right, though the weak point is, as often, to be sought not so much in the theory as in the man behind the theory. We shall come upon it as we examine what he meant by this "art" without which natural gifts are wasted.

Besides "nature," three things help, he says, to form the poet: "exercise, imitation and study;"[4] and these he considers in order.

By "exercise" he means patient labor towards perfection of form, the Horatian idea, expressed, however, with a delightful touch of true English humor:

"Try another time with labor. If then it succeed not, cast not away the quills yet, nor scratch the wainscot, beat not the poor desk, but bring all to the forge and file again; torn it anew. There is no statute law of the kingdom bids you be a poet against your will or the first quarter; if it comes in a year or two, it is well."[5]

---

[1] Ib.
[2] Ib., p. 73.
[3] Ib., p. 49.
[4] Ib., p. 75. Compare Sidney: *Defense of Poesy*, p. 46. Both are doubtless following Longinus.
[5] Ib., p. 76.

So far, good; but when he ends: " Indeed, things wrote with labor deserve to be so read and will last their age,"[1] we protest with a "*non sequitur.*" This it was which Jonson could never learn—that though perfection is scarcely to be attained without labor, it is not necessarily attained by it; that, even if the writer has patiently "forged" and "filed," it is often a far cry yet to immortality.

Jonson's use of the term "imitation" is noteworthy. He does not mean that the poet is to imitate nature, but that he shall "be able to convert the substance or riches of another poet to his own use. To make choice of one excellent man above the rest, and so to follow him till he grow very he, or so like him as the copy may be mistaken for the principal."[2] Here he is closely following Longinus, though he has failed to catch the poetic fervor of his original and so has lost a little of its truth. Compare this passage:

> We may learn from this author [Plato], if we would but observe his example, that there is yet another path besides those mentioned which leads to sublime heights. What path do I mean? The emulous imitation of the great poets and prose writers of the past. On this mark, dear friend, let us keep our eyes ever steadfastly fixed. Many gather the divine impulse from another's spirt, just as we are told that the Pythian priestess, when she takes her seat on the tripod, where there is said to be a rent in the ground breathing upward a heavenly emanation, straightway conceives from that source the godlike gift of prophecy and utters her inspired oracles, so likewise from the mighty genius of the great writers of antiquity there is carried into the souls of their rivals, as from a fount of inspiration, an effluence which breathes upon them until, even though their natural temper be but cold, they share the sublime enthusiasm of others."[3]

The fact that in dealing with this all-important phrase "imitation of nature," Jonson turned from Aristotle to Longinus—from the philosopher and nature-lover to the rhetorician and book-lover—is an interesting illus-

---

[1] Ib., p. 77.
[2] Ib.
[3] Longinus: *On the Sublime*, p. 29.

tration of the truth that we get out of books mainly what we bring to them. It is only in the present century that we have grown able to give understanding attention to those profound first chapters in the *Poetics*, where the relations between art and nature, between comedy and tragedy, are touched upon. One would like to have had Jonson's comment on Aristotle's dictum that comedy presents men as worse than they are,[1] and on this statement of tragic "imitation":

"They (portrait painters), while reproducing the distinctive form of the original, make a likeness which is true to life and yet more beautiful. So too the poet . . . . should preserve the type and yet ennoble it."[2]

But for thinking along these lines and in this manner the time was not yet ripe, and it was, we repeat, most significant that with a fundamental problem of art staring him in the face, Jonson should have placidly ignored it, and been content to adopt a use of the term "imitation" which transferred its application from a study of nature—Aristotle's meaning—to a study of books—Longinus' meaning. It was a sign of advance when Dryden, stimulated by French criticism, seriously took up the question, for though his treatment of it was shifting and superficial, the recognition of it as a problem at all marked a step forward on the path of literary æsthetics.

Yet a third thing, in Jonson's opinion, is needed for the poet's education:

"But that which we especially require in him, is an exactness of study, and multiplicity of reading, *lectio*, which maketh a full man."[3]

True, again; yet one cannot help feeling that what was true from the pen of his contemporary, the scientist-philosopher, was not so true from that of the scholar-

---

[1] Aristotle: *Poetics*, II, 4.
[2] Ib., XV, 8.
[3] *Timber*, p. 77.

poet. He would, of course, never have explicitly stated that it was reading and reading alone that made the full man; yet one feels that this was a blunder he instinctively fell into, and that it was this mistake, grounded in his feeling rather than in his reasoning, that blinded him to the poverty of some scenes in his *Sejanus*, and of the greater part of his *Catiline*.

We have, then, Jonson's ideal poet, the man whose birth "doth ask an age," of lofty morality, whose rare natural endowments have been refined and perfected by "exercise, imitation and study." In a word, we have a portrait of Jonson himself, very honestly given, too, with the faults on the surface, as we have seen. In fact, he scarcely does himself justice, for he leaves out of account—unless he meant to imply it in this unfortunately vague term 'nature'—the hold on human life which he must have had who could produce such characters as Rabbi Busy and Ursula, Sir Epicure Mammon and Volpone.

If Jonson's love of the written page was sometimes his weakness, it was in another way his strength. Schelling, in his introduction to *Timber*, suggests that "the conscious cultivation of English prose style began to be practiced at least a generation before Abraham Cowley and John Dryden."[1] This is scarcely going far enough, for the 'conscious cultivation of prose style' had begun even before Lyly, whose worst extravagance was only the *reductio ad absurdum* of prevailing tendencies from which even Sidney was not wholly free. Jonson's merit is that he helped to bring the language out of the *cul de sac* into which this had led it, and set it on the high road of its true development. It was not merely his sensitiveness to the beauty of words in themselves, though this too he had:

---

[1] *Timber*, Introduction, p. xxv.

"Some words are to be culled out for ornament and color, as we gather flowers to straw houses or make garlands; but they are better when they grow to our style as in a meadow, where, though the mere grass and greenness delights, yet the variety of flowers doth heighten and beautify."[1]

For delightful as "mere grass and greenness" is, there was perhaps a little too much of it in the Elizabethan writing. Nor was it simply the rhetorician's feeling for language, though that was strong in him, distinguishing "what word is proper, which hath ornament, which height, what is beautifully translated, where figures are fit, which gentle, which strong."[2] It was the sense for what may be called the architectonics of style, such as inspired these words:

"The congruent and harmonious fitting of parts in a sentence hath almost the fastening and force of knitting and connection; as in stones well squared, which will rise strong a great way without mortar."[3]

Perhaps no figure has ever expressed more happily the impression that a certain kind of excellence of style, in any language, makes upon us. As he wrote that, we may be sure that he had in mind besides the Latin classics, the example of two men, himself and Bacon. He could scarcely have had better models, and through them he got at one of the fundamental principles of good prose. Of a more delicate temper is this:

"Periods are beautiful when they are not too long; for so they have their strength too, as in a pike or javelin."[4]

Pater might have said that, though only the best of Pater's own writing conforms to it:

Such ideas, expressed with such beautiful adequacy, show what his own "imitation" had done for Jonson himself. His rare scholarship and fine appreciation of

---

[1] Ib., pp. 61, 62.
[2] Ib., pp. 27.
[3] Ib., p. 62.
[4] Ib., p. 62.

the best authors had taught him "not to imitate servilely, as Horace saith, and catch at vices for virtue," and his prose, with Bacon's, must have gone far towards establishing a norm of style, not imitated from but inspired by the best work of the ancient world, and catching some of its dignity and simplicity;—a style which led the way to the prose of Milton and Dryden and Congreve.

"Most loving of antiquity" as he was, it is the more surprising to find his attitude toward classic standards characterized by a sturdy independence of authority as such which is truly English and as truly modern. A manly discipleship leading to a manly self-reliance, this was his ideal:

"Besides, as it is fit for grown and able writers to stand of themselves, and work with their own strength, to trust and endeavor by their own faculties, so it is fit for the beginner and learner to study others and the best."[1]

Of Aristotle he was not the blind worshiper but the reasoning and discriminating, if enthusiastic, follower. Nothing can be better, either in style or temper, than the passages where he defends his position; there needs no apology for the length of the quotations.

"I am not of that opinion to conclude a poet's liberty within the narrow limits of laws which either the grammarians or philosophers prescribe. For before they found out those laws there were many excellent poets that fulfilled them, amongst whom none more perfect than Sophocles, who lived a little before Aristotle. Which of the Greeklings durst ever give precepts to Demosthenes? or to Pericles, whom the age surnamed Heavenly, because he seemed to thunder and lighten with his language? or to Alcibiades, who had rather Nature for his guide than Art for his master?"[2]

"*Non nimium credendum antiquitati.*—I know nothing can conduce more to letters than to examine the writings of the ancients,

---

[1] Ib., p. 55.
[2] Ib., pp. 79, 80.

and not to rest in their sole authority, or take all upon trust from them, provided the plagues of judging and pronouncing against them be away; such as are envy, bitterness, precipitation, impudence, and scurrile scoffing. For to all the observations of the ancients we have our own experience, which if we will use and apply, we have better means to pronounce. It is true they opened the gates and made the way that went before us, but as guides, not commanders: *Non domini nostri, sed duces fuere.* Truth lies open to all; it is no man's several. *Patet omnibus veritas; nondum est occupata. Multum ex illa, etiam futuris relictum est.*[1]

Nothing is more ridiculous than to make an author a dictator, as the schools have done Aristotle. The damage is infinite knowledge receives by it; for to many things a man should owe but a temporary belief, and a suspension of his own judgment, not an absolute resignation of himself, or a perpetual captivity. Let Aristotle and others have their dues; but if we can make farther discoveries of truth and fitness than they, why are we envied?"[2]

In such passages Jonson is at his best. Sane and yet bold, trenchant and yet temperate, he gets at the root of the matter, and his conservatism, well marked as it is, is a rational conservatism, quite distinct from the fanatical devotion to the past which prevailed in France throughout the sixteenth century.

Not that he undervalued the great philosopher. "Aristotle," he says, "was the first accurate critic and truest judge, nay, the greatest philosopher the world ever had.[3] And he says elsewhere: "Let us beware, while we strive to add, we do not diminish or deface."[4] But he claimed the right of free thought in the realm of letters as others had claimed it in the domain of religion, and if he made few departures from classic practice this was because he had given to the classic standards his independent and deliberate assent. It was with him a question not of authorities but of truth.

"I do not desire," he says, "to be equal to those that went before; but to have my reason examined with theirs, and so much faith to

---

[1] Ib., p. 7.
[2] Ib., p. 66.
[3] Ib., p. 78.
[4] Ib., p. 66.

be given them, or me, as those shall evict. I am neither author nor fautor of any sect. I will have no man addict himself to me; but if I have anything right, defend it as Truth's, not mine. . . . . Stand for truth, and 'tis enough: *Non mihi cedendum, sed veritati.*"[1]

In this last phrase is the conclusion of the whole matter—"*Non mihi cedendum, sed veritati*"; for one feels that his devotion to the classics is indeed the result of a devotion to truth as he saw it, not to a convention or a tradition.

In the rules that he gives for dramatic writing we get what is virtually a résumé of some of the most striking parts of the *Poetics*. Thus, he says that the poem must have "one entire and perfect action,"[2] that is, it must have "a beginning, a midst, and an end,"[3] its range should be neither too large nor too restricted, so it "exceed not the compass of one day." It is deeply interesting to see how thoroughly the poet has mastered this part of the treatise, and how he passes from point to point, condensing here, amplifying there, often supplying a particular illustration where the Greek had used a general statement, and always rendering the spirit as well as the letter of his original. He feels the force, for instance, of Aristotle's insistence on an inner and organic, as distinct from a superficial unity; and while in prescribing the unity of time he transforms into a positive requirement Aristotle's somewhat careless and wholly undogmatic generalization from Greek usage, he does not follow this up, as the French did, by insisting on unity of place, which Aristotle does not even mention.

In Jonson's own comedies[4] he adheres rather carefully to the unity of time, while in one, "*The Alchemist*," his conformity to the unity of place is such as even Corneille would scarcely have accused of "license."[5] For

---
[1] Ib., p. 8. Schelling has "veritate," doubtless a misprint.
[2] Ib., p. 84.
[3] Ib.
[4] Except *The Case Is Altered*, which is, of course, always to be excepted in any such statements as to Jonson's usage.
[5] Cf. Corneille: Discours III, *Des Trois Unités*.

the most part, however, he seems to have been satisfied with confining his action to a single city or its environs. As to unity of action, he works with a very free—almost too free—hand, in marked contrast to Molière, some of whose plays remind one of Schopenhauer's criticism of French tragedies " which in general observe this (unity) so strictly that the course of the drama is like a geometrical line without breadth. There it is constantly a case of 'Only get on! Pensez a votre affaire!'"[1] And whatever perfection of modelling and power of appeal Molière gains by this singleness of aim, Jonson's method has its own virtues of breadth and mass.[2]

But it is interesting to find that while in his comedies Jonson was thus regular, his usage as a tragedian is different: *Sejanus* breaks the unity of time, *Catiline* conforms neither in place nor time. The noteworthy thing is that in thus setting at naught a rule he had himself enunciated Jonson was conforming to a higher law, founded on a fundamental distinction between comedy and tragedy. The essence of the tragic lies in the clash between will and law, it is found in "the fatality of the consequences which follow upon every human act."[3] Now the essence of the comic, whatever it may be, is surely not that. For comedy deals with the aspects of things, often taken very arbitrarily and in a sense very superficially—and rightly so, else there is danger of trenching on the tragic. It is, then, necessarily a thing of the moment, it has no past and no future, and in a play to which it gives the stamp it is natural though not necessary that the action should have a brief range. Tragedy, on the other hand, is essentially grounded in time, and the so-called "tragic incongruity" is not tragic by virtue of its incongruity considered apart. Hamlet face to face with the unknown may—Mr. Dowden notwithstanding[4]—be as legitimately a comic as a

---

[1] Schopenhauer: *The World as Will and Idea*, III, 216.
[2] Cf. the discussion of *Every Man in His Humour*, infra pp. 46-ff.
[3] Amiel: *Journal*, April 6, 1851.
[4] Dowden: *Shakspere—His Mind and Art*, p. 352.

tragic spectacle; it is when one views him as a nucleus of causes and results that the tragic element appears. For its source is not in juxtaposition but in movement, in struggle; it has, in a word, development.[1] That many comedies violate the unities and many tragedies observe them, proves nothing. In Shakespeare's comedies, for example, the extension in time has to do with the serious plots of the plays, it does not affect the comic scenes, which are set like so many separate pictures,—or in which, we may say more truly, the poet relinquishes for the moment the serious attitude and chooses to look at things for their superficial incongruities.[2] The events of a tragedy, on the other hand, can indeed be compressed into a brief time; we do not deny this, only maintaining that the time element is necessary. For even in such a tragedy as *Oedipus King*, where the action covers only a few hours, it is not until we have in spirit lived over a life's past, and felt forward into its future, that we get the bitterness of the tragedy crushed into those few hours.

Jonson's usage in his comedy and his tragedy becomes thus very significant. For, especially in the case of *Sejanus*—which, despite the critics, seems in many ways a very wonderful play—he would have lost greatly in effectiveness if he had tried to force the action into narrower limits. The play is built up round the two titanic figures, Sejanus and Tiberius, and its tragic forces are found in the development of the inner purposes of these two, out of a state of harmony into one of complete and deadly opposition, ending in the final overthrow of the favorite. Such a theme could scarcely have been treated in any shorter time than Jonson has given it, and that he felt this and conformed, consciously or unconsciously, to a higher than the written law, is a sign of his real greatness.

---

[1] In this connection, Cf. infra pp. 37-8
[2] Cf. Everett: *Poetry, Comedy and Duty*, Chap. II.

In studying Jonson's literary theory one is impressed by two things. First, one is surprised at the extent to which he had assimilated the Greek æsthetics, as embodied in Aristotle, so far as they touched upon questions of poetic form. In his interpretation of the *Poetics* he might have given lessons to Corneille and to Dryden. One has only to compare, for example, the utterances in *Timber* with those in Corneille's essays on the three unities, to see the difference between thinking that is vital, if crude, and thinking that is shackled with conventions. Second, one feels more and more strongly as one's acquaintance with him deepens, that while as regards form his theory was Greek in its reasonable temperateness, he was himself by temperament a Roman of the stoic type. More than enough has been said of his borrowing from antiquity, but what has not been sufficiently emphasized is the intellectual processes behind this "borrowing," which determine its significance. He did not copy the Roman writers, he identified himself with them; he did not steal their thoughts, he thought them and felt them; and when he used their words it was because no fitter ones would naturally occur to him. In the *Timber*, as elsewhere, one passes from Jonson to Seneca and back to Jonson without consciousness of a transition, and it is no discredit even to the critical reader if he now and then takes for Jonson's own some passage that is really a translation or a paraphrase from a Roman classic. In a genuine sense, the thought is really Jonson's own, being made so by right of complete assimilation. Therefore what might have been pedantry in another is natural and legitimate in him. Not that he was wholly free from pedantry, but his undeniable vanity with regard to his classic learning has created a false impression that he was only a copyist. Thus, in *Sejanus* the array of references in the foot-notes is calculated to make one assume that the whole thing is a transcript from the Roman writers. In one sense, this is the case, but if one goes to the sources thus pointed out, one finds that the entire mass of his material has been worked over and scarcely is one stone left upon another. There is, it is true, hardly an incident of importance in his play which cannot be found in Suetonius, or Tacitus, or Dion Cassius; but his arrangement, his elaboration, his emphasis, his selection —all these are his own. In a few instances he has transferred a huge block of material from Tacitus to his own play;[1] for the rest, he has simply saturated himself with the spirit of the period he is writing about—"sich darin eingelebt"—so that his play, though for many reasons not a model tragedy, seems to have been, not copied from Tacitus, but written with the spirit of Tacitus upon him.

No one can study Jonson's theory as set forth in *Timber* and interpreted by his other works, without wonder at his power, his breadth, his grip on vital issues. And the more one perceives this, the more one feels the essential contrast between his mind and Dryden's, whose catholicity of taste and breadth of literary philosophy seems in part only one phase of a vacillating impressibility due to the want of a central point of view. This central point of view Jonson had attained, and it is for this reason that his *Timber*, despite its apparent lack of order, makes upon us the impression of a unified whole. Nor is his the superficial consistency of a narrow mind. His perception that truth is higher than authority, that laws are generalizations, not causes, his suggestion of the historic method in dealing with antiquity, prove him a philosophic and vital thinker. And when we call him a classicist we are right only if we recognize the term in its best significance—as the symbol not of a narrow and mechanical scholasticism but of a legitimate and honorable mode of thought based on a perception of the beauty of order and symetry in the things of the imagination as in the things of the reason.

---

[1] He does this in the speeches of Tiberius and some of those of Sejanus, and in the long defense of Cremutius Cordus; these are all.

CHAPTER II.

The Comedian's Material and His Attitude.

In one of Jonson's plays, the revellers, borrowing of the gods their names and powers, gather round the banquet-table and with Jove at their head hold Olympian festival. In the midst there breaks in the earthly monarch, imperial Cæsar, and the "quire of gods" is confounded. Even so does Jonson appear late among the Elizabethan poets, and even so does he scorn their divinity in his sentence: "Men are decayed, and studies,"[1] even so does he ignore it in his contempt for a world that he deems "sick and infirm," whose "old age itself is a disease."[2]

In thus drawing apart from his fellows Jonson challenges with peculiar directness the judgment of all who love the literature of the age he condemned. How far was he right in his condemnation? Wherein was he different from the rest? Which could most truly claim divinity? What must be our final estimate of him? It is in attempting to answer such questions as these that the following pages have been written.

It is unfortunate that we have but the one word—comedy—by which to designate many things. It serves to denote alike the comic element in a play, or the play itself of which the comic element may be but a small part; we use it to designate in turn the work of Shakespeare, of Jonson, of Aristophanes. Yet the huge laughter of the Greek, and its reckless abandonment; the "slim, feasting smile" of Molière; the chuckle of Lear's sad-eyed fool;—these are, it would seem, more diverse the one from the other than are some smiles from some

---
[1] *Timber*, p. 7.
[2] Ib., p. 12.

tears. We feel this, yet the name of comedy clings to them all, and it is perhaps partly this accident of a common title that has led critics to talk of Shakespeare and Jonson and Aristophanes as if they could be reduced to a single term and judged by a single standard.

Certain things, indeed, they do have in common. The comic standpoint always has a certain detachedness of view, in virtue of which one stands off from the object and perceives its incongruities as such, and the basis of all comedy is this perception of incongruity. The basis of dramatic comedy in particular is a perception of the incongruities found in human life, for those comic effects whose material is words and concepts and which are roughly designated by the term *wit*, are not distinctively dramatic but belong to all forms of literary expression.

Dramatic comedy, then, dealing with the comic aspect of human life, may be considered in two ways: with reference to its material, or with reference to the author's attitude. As to its material, there are two realms of comic effect furnished by life: those of incident and of character. As to the author's attitude, he may view his material with a regard varying between the sympathetic and the satiric, and he may see in his subject the individual, or the type, or the one in the other. Our final judgment of a comedy will be determined by our judgment of it in these two ways.

The distinction between incident and character may, indeed, be objected to on several grounds. Henry James does object to it. "What is character," he says, "but the determination of incident? What is incident but the illustration of character?"[1] Yet though this is as true of some comedy as it is in novel-writing about which he is talking, it is not true of all. There are comedies of incident with no differentation of character whatever, or only the most conventional sort;

---

[1] Henry James: *The Art of Fiction*, p. 69.

and there are comedies where the weight of emphasis at least is on the exposition of characters, who stand still and pose to be drawn. The two kinds of effects may be found in a primitive form in our modern variety show. Here a mad succession of surprising tumbles, beatings, whacks on the head and trippings-up of the feet of the comic butt, is planned to keep the audience in a roar. It does not matter what sort of person he is to whom these things happen; the emphasis is on the event itself, not on the character of the recipient, and the comic element is found in the incongruity between anticipation and actual occurrence. On the other hand the laughter that arises at sight of the huge, misshapen figure of some made-up monstrosity has a slightly different source: it is based in the perception of a departure from some standard, which is assumed as the norm. The fat or the thin man the very tall or very short man, is funny not in himself, but when mentally compared with the normal man who is neither fat nor thin, neither tall nor short. Place the tall and the short man side by side and the comic effect is heightened by the double comparison instantly suggested. Yet the juxtaposition of a normal man and a child is not funny, although the disproportion is as great, because between them there is no common standard by which we can measure them; each conforms to his own norm. But let the child attempt to assume the airs of a man, and the result is comic, because in so doing he has brought upon himself the application of the man's standard, and his departure from that standard is seized upon by the comic sense. Thus it appears that the essential element in comic perception of this sort is a recognized norm, by reference to which the incongruity is perceived. Falstaff, always alive to the comic in himself, perfectly grasps the principle of comic effect when he turns in mock fury upon his diminutive page with: " I do here walk before thee like a sow that hath overwhelmed all her litter but one. If the prince put thee into my service for any other reason than to set me off, why then I have no judgment."[1]

What is true of the physical realm is equally true of the spiritual, and the comic treatment of character can be reduced to the same principle as the comic use of deformity. It is the defects in men that the comedian seizes upon, the places in their spiritual build where they are disproportioned, overgrown or undergrown, and the treatment of Falstaff's physical deformities has the same basis as the treatment of Malvolio's spiritual ones.

Neither Falstaff nor Malvolio, however, are as far toward the character-end of the scale as, for example, *The Comedy of Errors* is toward the incident-end. For incident may be presented without character, but character may scarcely be presented dramatically save through incident, and in most comedy the two things are inextricably bound up together: the incidents depend for their comic quality on the character of the participants in them, the comic aspects of the characters are made apparent through the incidents. Yet there is this difference between the mutual relations of these two elements in Shakespeare and in Jonson: Shakespeare seems to have taken his plots pretty well made up, and to have created his characters within their lines, thus vivifying and transforming the original story; Jonson's plays, on the other hand, give an impression of being built up in a fashion the very reverse of this: it seems—if we may roughly indicate what must have been really a very complex process—as if he had first selected his characters and then worked out to fit them a plot such as would best show off their qualities. The result is seen in the difference between Shakespeare's plots and Jonson's—a difference that will be discussed later on.

Admitting, then, that strictly speaking plot and character ought not to be considered apart from one

---
[1] *Henry IV*, Part II; Act 1, Sc. 2.

another, we have for convenience, ventured to treat them separately, considering first the characters, and then the plot as determined by the characters.

The characteristic of the comic standpoint being its regard for incongruities as such, the material for it in human nature will be found, as already stated, in the imperfections of men's character. A perfectly poised character, one absolutely symmetrical, would not be comic. It might be involved from without in a comic situation, but the comic would be that of external incident, the character itself would be immune from the comedian's touch. But as soon as any defect is seen, any lack of proportion, the opportunity is given, the material is liable to be seized upon. Nothing can be better than Meredith's words regarding this phase of the comic spirit:

> "Men's future upon earth does not attract it; their honesty and shapeliness in the present does; and whenever they wax out of proportion, overblown, affected, pretentious, bombastical, hypocritical, pedantic, fantastically delicate; whenever it sees them self-deceived or hoodwinked, given to run riot in idolatries, planning short-sightedly, plotting dementedly; whenever they are at variance with their professions, and violate the unwritten but perceptible laws binding them in consideration one to another; whenever they offend sound reason, fair justice; are false in humility or mined with conceit, individually, or in the bulk—the Spirit overhead will look humanely malign and cast an oblique light on them, followed by volleys of silvery laughter. That is the Comic Spirit." [1]

The first part of this passage, which has to do with the comedian's material, is applicable to all comic writing, from Aristophanes to Gilbert. But the last phrases, which in an exquisite figure seek to express the attitude of the comedian toward his material, though beautifully appropriate when applied, as Meredith meant them, to Molière, cannot be used of other comedians. The laughter of Aristophanes is seldom "silvery"; the laughter of Shakespeare is sometimes

---
[1] Meredith: *An Essay on Comedy*, pp. 83, 84.

tempered, though not checked, by keenest pity; the laughter of Jonson is often not thoroughly "humane." It is at this point that comedians diverge, and their writings fall into groups; the basic material is the same, but the attitude varies. For obviously it is possible, while perceiving the comic aspect of human infirmities, to pity these infirmities, or to regard them indulgently, or to deride them, or to launch against them the bitterest invective, or, finally, to regard them without passing judgment at all. According as the writer's attitude is or is not, on the whole, one of censure, comedies fall into two classes which we may call judicial and non-judicial; the judicial is apt to pass over into satire, the non-judicial into pathos. The difference between the two attitudes may be illustrated by the difference between Shakespeare's treatment of Malvolio and of Falstaff; it is indicated, too, in the shades of difference between the treatment of Falstaff in *The Merrry Wives of Windsor* and in *Henry IV*. We recognize that the Malvolio episodes, and those of *The Merry Wives* are less Shakespearean than those of *Henry IV*, and we may accept Shakespeare as representative of the non-judicial type.

The judicial, the satiric, is the older sort. In Greece comedy arose out of satire of the most direct and intimate character, and Aristophanes' satire is still recklessly personal and deliberately judicial and didactic. In Menander it became more general, levelling its judgments at types instead of at individuals, and it was this note that Terence took up for the Roman Comedy. That comedy ought explicitly to judge, to teach, to, exhort was accepted as a fundamental principle, and Sidney was expressing the traditional creed when he said:

"The comedy is an imitation of the common errors of our life, which he representeth in the most ridiculous and scornful sort that may be, so as it is impossible that any beholder can be content to be such a one."[1]

---
[1] Sidney: *Defense of Poesy*, p. 28.

The passage exactly illustrates the comic satirist's position: "The common errors of our life" describes his material; "the most ridiculous and scornful sort that may be," covers the treatment; and the last clause, "so as it is impossible that any beholder can be content to be such a one," states the underlying purpose, as comedians have usually asserted it. It exactly applies to Jonson; it does not apply at all to Shakespeare's mature work, which we must always regret that Sidney did not see.

It is, therefore, not with Shakespeare that Jonson must be compared, but with Aristophanes, Menander, Terence, among the ancients, and, among the moderns, with Molière and with the English comedy of which Congreve is the most brilliant representative. All of these are judicial, all are satiric, some of them are in spirit far more nearly akin to Juvenal and Swift than to Shakespeare, and one feels that the classification which throws Jonson with Shakespeare, instead of with Juvenal, and puts Tacitus into yet another group,—that such a classification has its weak points.

For with Jonson's and Sidney's point of view it is apparent that we are approaching very close to satire, and that it depends less on the theory than on the temper of the writer and the character of his times, whether he will express his thought in satiric dramas or satiric histories or satiric epistles. Moreover, no division line can be drawn between the comedian with satiric color, and the satirist whose comic sense has hardened to irony, and the aim here is not to establish boundaries but to discover tendencies.

CHAPTER III.

CHARACTER TREATMENT IN JONSON'S TYPICAL COMEDY.

Accepting, then, Jonson's work as of the judicial type, consider in detail his treatment of character. And first, it does not do to rest upon his own assertions with regard to his writing. For, with the best intentions, one seldom tells the exact truth about oneself, and though what a man says of himself is always significant and worth regarding, it is often to be taken as indirectly indicative of his real nature and purpose rather than as directly descriptive of them. Jonson, moreover, was sometimes singularly infelicitous in speaking of himself, and the mere culling from prologue and epilogue of all the lines in which he expresses his dramatic theory will not give quite an adequate conception of his actual work. Especially is this true of his comedies, where his artistic sense sometimes led him to depart as a playwright from some of his theories as a thinker. It was not that his utterances were insincere, but that his theory was not quite complete enough to cover all of his practice.

This method of collecting his statements and adding them together to stand for his art is perhaps responsible for the assumption generally made that Jonson's comedies always enforce a moral lesson. This is simply not true, although he himself does with great emphasis and entire sincerity assert that the duty of the comedian is to punish vice. Thus here:

> " But with an armed and resolved hand,
> I'll strip the ragged follies of the time
> Naked as at their birth . . . .
> . . . . and with a whip of steel,
> Print wounding lashes in their iron ribs.

. . . . my strict hand
Was made to seize on vice, and with a gripe
Squeeze out the humor of such spongy souls,
As lick up every idle vanity." [1]

This is well enough for a part of his work. It applies to *Volpone;* it applies also to *The Poetaster* and to *Cynthia's Revels*, though not in the same sense, for the genuine morality of *Volpone* is as diverse as possible from the pharisaic, egotistic superiority of the last two plays. It applies also to Jonson's two tragedies, and to parts of his other comedies. On the other hand, the moral of *The Alchemist* or of *Bartholomew Fair* would be hard to find. For Jonson did indeed teach and scourge, but not always did his teaching inculcate morality or his scourging lash the scoundrel as such. On the whole, his efforts are directed quite as much against intellectual weakness as against moral, and he preached quite as emphatically from the text "don't be a fool" as from the text "don't be a knave," while if we except his tragedies, the weight of emphasis is rather on the first than on the second. Run rapidly through the important plays with this in view:

In *Every Man in His Humour* there are a number of rogues and a few honest men, but the line of division is drawn, not on a basis of honesty, but on a basis of wit. The three witty rogues, Wellbred, Young Knowell, and Brainworm, are successful in discomfiting not only the other rogues, but also the honest men, and Brainworm is at the end pardoned for his offenses because he has shown such ability in committing them. Such a play can scarcely be called moral, though no one would call it immoral either, unless it were some zealot such as Zeal-of-the-land Busy. If it teaches anything, it teaches that it is convenient to have a quick brain, a ready tongue, and an elastic conscience.

In *Every Man out of His Humour* the tone is more severe, and the author, speaking through Macilente,

---
[1] Induction, *Every Man out of His Humour;* Works, II, 12, 18.

does indeed lash vice as well as folly. Every person is in turn exposed and censured, but the moral tone is spoiled by the fact that Macilente himself, through whose malignant activity these exposures are brought about, is left untouched. He is rather the most disagreeable scoundrel of them all, yet he goes free, and leaves the stage at the end licking his chops over the discomfiture he has occasioned.

In *Cynthia's Revels* and *The Poetaster* the pharisaic tone already alluded to may be called moral, but it seems more truly immoral than the most direct praise of vice could be.

Sejanus and *Volpone*, which follow, may be taken together, though one is called tragedy and one comedy. In these the tone, for the first and almost the last time, is that of a firm and strenuous morality. Both plays show stupendous vice bringing upon itself its own ruin—a negative kind of morality, to be sure, but genuine and consistent.

In *Epicoene*, however, we have pure farce, without a trace of moral tone, and all the better for its freedom from it, and in *The Alchemist* we have the very apotheosis of roguery. Three people conspire to cheat the world. Their success is complete and they outwit the vicious, the hypocritical, the simple; but they also bring about the discomfiture of the only honest man in the play. When at last they are brought to bay, one of the three saves himself by deserting the other two, and purchases his master's forgiveness by making over to him their ill-gotten gains.

Finally, in the coarse but good-natured laughter of *Bartholomew Fair*, even the fools are let off easily, while the knaves find the mad, merry rascality of the fair a very Elysium. One might go on through the rest of the plays, but the great ones end here, and the rest would not furnish anything new.

Jonson's comedy, then, is judicial but not always moral, that is, it always subjects its persons to a judgment according to some standard, but this standard is quite as apt to be an intellectual one as a moral one. Among those which apply an intellectual standard, *The Alchemist* and *Bartholomew Fair* are preëminent; among those which apply the moral standard, *Volpone* stands alone among the comedies, but in this as in other respects it may be classed with the tragedies *Sejanus* and *Catiline*.

Thus far we have been considering the general tone and purpose of the comedies in their treatment of character. The next question is as to the method of treatment. Satire, Moulton remarks, may accomplish its end in one of two ways; "the one declares a thing ridiculous, the other exhibits it in a ridiculous disguise. Reducing the two to their lowest terms, in the one you call a man a fool, in the other you disguise yourself in his likeness and then play the fool"—he illustrates by citing the *Saturday Review* and *Punch*, "the first alleges folly, the latter presents it."[1]

In the case of the dramatist, one would suppose that only the second method would be employed. As a matter of fact the temptation to "allege" folly as well to "present" it is usually too great to be resisted. Even Molière sometimes has a wise Dorine or a Cléante to explain or expose the follies of the other characters, while Jonson almost always has some such character to stand, as it were, with pointer in hand, as demonstrator of the action. Once one begins to watch for this feature it is really remarkable how constant it is. Sometimes there is one demonstrator for the entire play, sometimes there are several who take turns. Thus, in *Every Man out of His Humour* Macilente is demonstrator in chief; for the scenes where he is absent, Carlo Buffone acts as understudy.[2] In *Cynthia's Revels*, Crites holds the pointer;[3] in *The Poetaster*, it is Horace; in *The Silent*

---
[1] Moulton: *The Ancient Classical Drama*, p. 256.
[2] Cf. infra, pp. 58-60.
[3] Mercury & Cupid are assistant-demonstrators; cf. infra, p. 83.

Woman, it is any one of the three friends: Truewit, Dauphine, or Clerimont; in *Volpone*, it is, for the main action, Mosca and Volpone themselves, who both egg on their victims and comment on their folly, while for the sub-interest of Sir Politick Would-be, the demonstrator or showman is Peregrine. Even Jonson's tragedy is not free from this peculiarity, for in *Sejanus* the function of Arruntius in the play is only as a commenter on the other characters.

Such an expedient seems essentially undramatic. When used to excess, as Jonson often used it, it is so. To be constantly explaining the nature of the characters implies either that the dramatist does not trust the cogency of his presentation, or that he does not trust the perceptive powers of the audience. The latter alternative is in Jonson's case not unlikely, but it is also true that, save when he was at his very best, his genius was more expository than dramatic; his mind was more akin to Bacon's than to Shakespeare's, and it was possibly a little easier for him to explain in crisp phrase exactly how a man was a fool, than for him to give the man free scope to act according to his folly.[1] Some of the best things in his dramas are found in these non-dramatic lapses. In *Every Man out of His Humour*, for instance, in the scene where the scented courtier, Fastidious Brisk, meets the court lady, Saviolina, Macilente stands by watching, and one of his comments is worth all the rest of the scene put together. Fastidious, knowing the lady is about to enter, says, "A kind of affectionate reverence strikes me with a cold shivering, methinks." Macilente mutters sardonically: "I like such tempers well, as stand before their mistresses with fear and trembling; and before their Maker, like impudent mountains!"[2]

When the practise is not carried to excess, however, it is not out of place, but is entirely consistent with the

---

[1] Extreme instances of this are *Every Man out of His Humour* and *Cynthia's Revels*. Cf. infra, pp. 57-60; 82, 83.
[2] *Every Man out of His Humour*, Act III, Sc. 3; Works, II, 118.

spirit of this kind of comedy. For, as will more clearly appear in the discussion of plots, the characters in any such play may always be divided into two groups, a large group of victims, a small group of victimizers or intriguers who control events and search out ways to "gull" the victims. Such being the case, it is quite natural that they should at the same time laugh at and discuss their folly. Thus in *Volpone*, the comments of Mosca and his master on the stupid greed of the legacy-hunters are dramatically proper, whereas those of Peregrine on Sir Politick are doubtful. In *Epicoene* the gleeful asides of the three young men as they work up the two fools, Daw and La-Foole, are as legitimate as are the whispered gibes of Sir Toby, Sir Andrew and Maria as they watch Malvolio from their ambush.

In his treatment of character, there are two dangers liable to beset the satiric dramatist. His material being human infirmity, his tone judicial and didactic, his temper a little superior if not scornful, he is apt to do one of two things:—if he is not broad-minded enough and impersonal enough he will be too particular, and fall into personal invective; if he has not a firm grasp of the concrete or artistic he will be too general, and will trench upon allegory.

The tendency toward personalities is easy to comprehend. It characterized the beginnings of comedy, and Aristophanes boldly and deliberately gave way to it. Menander appears to have broken away from it,—partly probably for political reasons,—and the Roman comedy is to some extent free from it, but it has always been one of the pitfalls of satire. Jonson certainly fell into it in two plays, *Cynthia's Revels* and *The Poetaster*, and probably in some parts of many of his other plays, and though he is vehement in defending himself from the charge of personality, his very defences, like his repeated assertions that he was above feeling the abuse of his enemies, do not leave upon us quite the impression he intended. Yet if this was his besetting sin, he knew it for a fault, knew that

> "poet never credit gain'd
> By writing truths, but things, like truths, well feign'd."[1]

And doubtless he was often enough misunderstood and wilfully misinterpreted. There were plenty of "small fry" about town, ready to "make a libel which he meant a play,"[2] and he has us heartily on his side when he scores the "State-decypherer, or politick picklock of the scene," who is "so solemnly ridiculous as to search out, who was meant by the gingerbread-woman, who by the hobby-horse man, who by the costard-monger, nay, who by their wares. Or that will pretend to affirm on his own inspired ignorance, what Mirror of Magistrate is meant by the justice, what great lady by the pig-woman, what concealed statesman by the seller of mouse-traps, and so of the rest."[3]

Compare with this an interesting parallel in Molière:

> "Et voilà de quoi j'ouïs l'autre jour se plaindre Molière, parlant à des personnes qui le chargeoient de même chose que vous. Il disoit que rien ne lui donnoit du déplaisir comme d'être accusé de regarder quelqu'un dans les portraits qu'il fait; que son dessein est de peindre les moeurs sans vouloir toucher aux personnes . . . . et que si quelque-chose étoit capable de le dégoûter de faire des comédies, c'étoit les ressemblances qu'on y vouloit toujours trouver," etc.[4]

While, for an agreement which was perhaps even deliberately verbal, note Congreve's:

> "Others there are, whose malice we'd prevent:
> Such, who watch plays, with scurrilous intent
> To mark out who by characters are meant:
> And though no perfect likeness they can trace,
> Yet each pretends to know the copied face.
> These, with false glosses, feed their own ill-nature,
> And turn to libel what was meant a satire."[5]

---

[1] Prologue, *The Silent Woman;* Works, III, 332.
[2] Ib. Cf. also in the Dedicatory Letter to *Volpone:* "I know that nothing can be so innocently writ or carried, but may be made obnoxious to construction," etc. Works. III, 158.
[3] Induction, *Bartholomew Fair;* Works IV, 353.
[4] Molière: *L'Impromptu de Versailles;* Oeuvres, III, 413.
[5] Congreve: Epilogue, *The Way of the World.*

The opposite tendency, that towards allegory, is a natural result of the comic point of view. For since the comedian regards defects, oddities of character, he is usually led to the study of temperaments in their extreme development, and his treatment is necessarily bound to emphasize the eccentricities in the temperament, leaving the rest of the personality somewhat shadowy. Indeed, it was a part of Jonson's theory that if eccentricity is anything more than external, it will effect the entire personality. To any such case he applies the term "humour," defining the term thus:

> "As when some one peculiar quality
> Doth so possess a man, that it doth draw
> All his affects, his spirits, and his powers,
> In their confluctions, all to run one way,
> This may be truly said to be a humor." [1]

The theory is physchologically perfectly sound, but it, as well as Jonson's practice, has met with rather harsh treatment at the hands of critics. Thus Hazlitt:

"His imagination fastens instinctively on some one mark or sign by which he designates the individual, and never lets it go, for fear of not meeting with any other means to express himself by. A cant phrase, an odd gesture, an old-fashioned regimental uniform, a wooden leg, a tobacco-box, or a hacked sword, are the standing topics by which he embodies his characters to the imagination." [2]

Such a statement simply showed that Hazlitt entirely missed the point of Jonson's work. Curiously enough, too, his criticism may be answered out of Jonson's own mouth, if we simply go on quoting the passage from *Every Man out of His Humour* begun above. The speaker, Asper, who represents Jonson, continues—give ear, Hazlitt—

> "But that a rook, by wearing a pyed feather,
> The cable hatband, or the three piled ruff,
> A yard of shoe-tye, or the Switzer's knot
> On his French garters, should affect a humor!
> O, it is more than most ridiculous." [3]

---

[1] Induction, *Every Man out of His Humour:* Works, II, 16.
[2] Hazlitt: *English Comic Writers*, 77.
[3] Ib., p. 17.

In other words, Jonson emphasizes the fact that it is inner and spiritual eccentricity with which he has to do, not accidents of external appearance.

Coleridge's censure touches him nearer, because it involves a truth, being scarcely more than a burlesque restatement of the above lines:

"Jonson's [characters] are either a man with a huge wen, having a circulation of its own, and which we might conceive amputated, and the patient thereby losing all his character; or they are mere wens themselves instead of men—wens personified, or with eyes, nose, and mouth cut out, mandrake fashion."[1]

Under the fantastic figure, Coleridge does here touch upon a real danger which besets all such writing—the danger of emphasizing a single odd trait to such an extent that the individual is lost sight of, or—which amounts to nearly the same thing—choosing as a subject for treatment some odd trait which is of so narrow a reach that it does not mold the rest of the character, but rather obscures it, and has the force of monomania, or "obsession." This is in fact a fault which Jonson's inferior work shows. Thus, the plot of *The Silent Woman* is based on a single characteristic of Morose, his hatred of noise. The play is, however, pure farce throughout, and as such the character of Morose is legitimate enough. If the play needed defense, however, the argument Gifford has chosen, if it were true, is the right one. He says:

"Both Upton and Whalley have mistaken the character of Morose, they suppose it to be a dislike of noise; whereas this is an accidental quality altogether dependent upon the master-passion, or 'humour,' a most inveterate and odious self-love."[2]

Even an admirer of Jonson may not quite agree with Gifford in this instance, but it is usually true that of Jonson's mature work Coleridge's criticism does not hold. In his three greatest plays, *The Alchemist*, *Volpone*,

---

[1] Coleridge: *Literary Remains*, II, 279.
[2] Gifford's note, *The Silent Woman*, III, 399.

and *Bartholomew Fair*, he never passes the bounds of the dramatic. *Bartholomew Fair* is the most concretely realistic piece of portraiture he ever did, *Volpone* deals more with generalized types, while *The Alchemist* stands between the two, but all keep within artistic limits.

In his less great work, however, the tendency to personification of single qualities is very clear. In *The Magnetic Lady*, for example, Lady Loadstone's powers of attraction are continually alluded to, though with no apparent reason unless it be perhaps the sound of her name, and at the end she is married to Captain Ironside, presumably because magnet attracts iron. In *The Staple of News* the symbolism is more than verbal, but is puzzlingly capricious. Pecunia is apparently an ordinary young lady, but occasionally she is made to stand for money or wealth taken allegorically, and though young Pennyboy assures us that "she kisses like a mortal creature" the reader is never quite clear in his mind as to whether she is a girl or a money-bag.[1]

These are extreme cases, but it would be possible to choose out characters from the plays so as to make a series illustrating steps in the process all the way from vivid artistic portraiture like that of the Puritan zealot in *Bartholomew Fair* to personification like that of Lady Pecunia, with her attendant maids, Mortgage, Statute, Band and Wax, and her gentleman-usher, Broker. Finally, it is interesting to note that the lapses into personification occur more frequently in his late plays, as his powers waned, while his over-personal invective appears to have come early, before he was inclined to control his resentments.

Another objection, most comprehensive of all, is made to comedy of the class to which Jonson's belongs. It is of Molière's plays, but it might as well be of Jonson's, that Freytag says:

---

[1] Cf. infra, pp. 90–92.

"The highest dramatic life is lacking to them—the processes of coming into being, the growth of character. We prefer to recognize on the stage how one *becomes* a miser, rather than how he *is* one."[1]

But this an indictment, not of Molière's or Jonson's comedy, but of all comedy. What we must look for in Jonson's comedies, as in Molière's, is a study not of character development but of characters which are already formed, or which are treated as if they were already formed. For, "how a man becomes a miser" is not a comic but a tragic spectacle. The essentially tragic in Browning's *A Soul's Tragedy* is the spectacle of Chiappino's degeneration; but a comedian might take up Chiappino where Browning left him, and make him the hero of a comedy like *Tartuffe*. He could not take the period of his life that Browning takes—the period of his "becoming" and treat it deeply or truly, without making it tragic.[2] Again, the history of Lydgate in *Middlemarch*, is, as it stands, a "soul's tragedy"; but the final Lydgate, the conventional, prosperous physician, specialist in gout, would furnish good material for the satiro-comic artist. And Tartuffe himself—would it have been comic to watch how he *became* Tartuffe? It is indeed true, as Hegel suggests, that to preserve the comic in a comedy we must drop the curtain in time. But it is perhaps equally true that we must, at its beginning, not raise the curtain too soon.

Of Jonson's five great plays the earliest has been called, perhaps rightly, his most perfect.[3] *Bartholomew Fair* is certainly the most recklessly, riotously funny, while *The Alchemist* and *Volpone* contend for the position of the greatest. *The Alchemist*, is, indeed, structurally the most marvelous of plays, but there are some readers at least with whom no comedy leaves the impression that *Volpone* does,—an impression comparable in inten-

---
[1] Freytag: *Technique of the Drama*, pp. 250, 251.
[2] Cf. Supra, pp. 17, 18. Note, however, that the process of reasoning does not imply any assertion that the converse is true: namely, that tragedy *must* involve character development. Few great tragedies have such a basis.
[3] Swinburne: *A Study of Ben Jonson*, pp. 3, 14.

sity with that made by a tragedy, though the effect here is mainly intellectual rather than emotional. It is the effect of the double character, Volpone-Mosca, which impresses us with a kind of hugeness, a diabolical fertility of power almost too great for comedy, and one cannot help wishing that Jonson had honored these two with opponents as worthy of their genius as those Shakespeare gave Iago.

Finally, to say that Jonson does not appeal to the imagination[1] is to forget Volpone, and Sir Epicure Mammon. What is true, is, that he appeals wholly to the intellect. Any one who expects to be emotionally touched will be disappointed, but if one is satisfied with the stimulus that comes of contact with a master mind, he will not seek in vain. Indeed one sometimes feels that, in coming from the sunny hedonism of some among the Elizabethans, there is a kind of pleasure, bracing while it chills, in getting into touch with this man, who stands apart from the rest, among them and not of them, whose "light" had not their "sweetness" and whose savage judgments never grew thoroughly humane, yet who had the nobleness that comes of power and sincerity and seriousness.

---

[1] Aronstein: *Ben Jonson's Theorie des Lustspiels; Anglia*, XVII, 477.

CHAPTER IV.

STRUCTURAL FEATURES OF JONSON'S TYPICAL COMEDY.

1. General Structure of the Satiro-comic Plot.

It was suggested in the preceding chapter that the relation of plot to character in Jonson's writing was the converse of what it was in Shakespeare's—that Jonson made his plots to fit his characters, while Shakespeare made his characters to fit his plots. A comparison of Shakespeare's plays with their sources in history or romance shows that he was at little trouble to alter his stories, and that the whole force of his genius went into a recreating of the persons in the story. The stories he chooses for his typical comedies are, moreover, serious love stories, and to this main interest the comic element is subordinated.

This comic element is introduced in two ways: through comic episodes interspersed between the serious scenes, and loosely connected with the main plot, and through a delicately comic treatment of the serious scenes themselves.

The first method is old—it goes back to the miracle plays; the second—the habit, namely, of treating a subject seriously and yet casting upon it a comic light—while it is found in other writers, has come to seem peculiarly Shakespearean, and it is one of the things that give to his three greatest comedies, *Much Ado About Nothing*, *As You Like It*, and *Twelfth Night*, their unique charm. The double point of view is embodied in his two most complex women characters, Rosalind and Beatrice, as its elements are singly projected, in *A Midsummer Night's Dream*, in the two beings, Oberon and Puck, Oberon taking the lover's mishaps seriously, Puck delighting in the comic aspect of them.

Structural Features of Jonson's Satiric Comedy. 41

Turning now to Jonson's typical comedies, we find something quite different. He starts with his group of characters whose comic aspects he wished to bring out. To this end he invents situations for them, and by combining these situations he gets a plot for the comedy. Thus, whereas in Shakespeare the serious interest determines the main plot and the comic interest is relegated to episodes or embodied in the treatment of the serious scenes, in Jonson the comic interest determines the main plot and the serious interest, where present, is subordinate. In Shakespeare the comic purpose influences the tone, the coloring, the atmosphere; in Jonson it not only does this but it actually prescribes the form, the underlying structure.

Naturally there results a complete divergence in the structural features of the two kinds of comedies. Shakespeare's plots have some resemblance to those of some tragedies, the difference being that, besides the happy ending, the incidents are more external, based rather on chance incident than on spiritual necessity. But even this distinction is in Shakespeare not always preserved. Compare, for example, the plots of *Romeo and Juliet* and *The Two Gentlemen of Verona*, which last we choose because of its simplicity. The story of *Romeo and Juliet* is as follows:

Two houses are involved in a deadly feud. Romeo, prince of one house, falls in love with Juliet, daughter of the opposing house. Juliet returns his love, but cannot free herself from parental tyranny, which is about to force her into a distasteful marriage. Romeo, because of an accidental street brawl, is banished. Juliet takes a sleeping potion which enables her to simulate death, and she is placed for dead in the family tomb. She has sent word to Romeo to come to the tomb and carry her away, but Romeo has missed her message and hearing only of the news of her death he returns to visit the tomb. He kills himself there, and she rouses from her lethargy to find his dead body beside her, whereupon she kills herself.

It will be seen that the story turns upon a series of accidents, and that it might as well have happened otherwise. Take now *The Two Gentlemen*.

Proteus is in love with Julia, a lady of Verona, and is loved by her, but his father sends him to Milan, and their intercourse is thus broken. At Milan he finds his friend Valentine wooing Silvia, daughter of the Duke. She returns his love, but her father opposes the marriage and favors another suitor. Proteus too falls in love with Silvia, and betrays to the Duke Valentine's plan to elope with his daughter. Valentine is thereupon banished, and Silvia yet more tyrannously urged on to the marriage with the favored suitor. Proteus takes advantage of the Duke's favor to press his own suit to Silvia, but his advances are met with reproachful contempt. Meanwhile Julia comes to Milan disguised as a page, to seek her lover. She enters his service and discovers his treachery. Silvia finally runs away to seek Valentine, and the Duke and Proteus, with Julia, pursue her. Proteus gets Silvia in his power but she is rescued by Valentine. He repents his treachery and renews allegiance to Julia, while Valentine is permitted to marry Silvia.

The resemblance of the Valentine-Silvia plot to the Romeo-Juliet one is manifest. It is equally manifest that there is no more reason why this plot should have made a comedy than why the other should have made a tragedy. A few changes toward the end would have made all the difference. In the treatment, however, there is no mistaking the difference of tone. The manner in the tragedy is consistently serious, there is no trace of the double attitude—the serious and the mocking—and the play is given an air of tragic necessity not inherent in the material. But structurally the two plays are of the same type: both show the growth of the bond between the lovers, then its severence through outside interference, then their separation, then their plan to be reunited. In the one case the plan, through a series of accidents, is successful; in the other, through a series of accidents, it fails.

Turn now to Jonson's plots. At first glance they seem too hopelessly complex for analysis, but, as will appear, their principle is single, and their underlying structure comparatively simple.

In discussing character it was remarked that Jonson's *dramatis personæ* could always be divided into two groups, a large group of victims and a small group of victimizers. It was also noted that Jonson shared the traditional view of comedy, i. e. that it should be such a "scornful" presentation of folly or vice as might deter men from falling into like errors. In his plays, accordingly, the victim-group presents to us the follies or vices chosen for treatment, the victimizer-group is entrusted with the duty of exploiting the owners of these follies and vices and bringing them to their natural end in exposure or ruin. The resulting plot may be briefly described as a network of practical jokes, some perfectly harmless, some more serious in their issues. There is no rise and fall of the movement, no action and reaction, such as we find in the serious drama and in the romantic comedy plots, there is simply the development of a trick or series of tricks, in which one set of participants are more or less helplessly passive, and the other set is mischievously or malignantly active.

Thus the Shakespeare type of comedy and the Jonson type are about as near two extremes as can be imagined. A middle form may be found, however, in the plays of Terence. These resemble Jonson's in the prominence given to trickery, but are like Shakespeare's in the fact that the tricks are for the most part not planned simply for trickery's sake, there is a serious purpose underlying all, which motives the action. Usually this is a love motive: e. g. a young man is in love with a slave-girl and wants to buy her freedom. He has no money and his father will not give him any. He therefore resorts to craft, and with the help of his servant succeeds in cozening the old man out of a large sum. Possibly it then transpires that the slave-girl is really the long lost daughter of a wealthy Athenian, and the young man is free to make so desirable an alliance. The wedding then occurs, all the trickery is forgiven and the young man's faithful if rascally servant receives his freedom.

This is not an exact summary of any single play, but may serve as a generalized type. It will be evident that such a plot contains the elements of both the kinds of comedy we have been discussing. Imagine the serious motive to be given great prominence while the comic trickery is made subordinate, and the resulting proportions might be those of the Romantic comedy. Indeed, the argument of some of Terence's plays as they stand might pass very well among these comedies; it is only in the treatment that the difference is brought out. Imagine, on the other hand, the serious motive in part or altogether suppressed, and the comic intrigue emphasized; the result will be comedy of Jonson's type. It is interesting to note that in Italy the drama seems actually to have passed through such modifications, the old Roman comedy developing on the one hand into Romantic love-drama, and on the other into the drama of comic intrigue.[1]

An English play which nearly preserves the Terentian proportions is Massinger's *A New Way to Pay Old Debts*. It is evidently derived from Middleton's *A Trick To Catch the Old One*, but the plot is greatly simplified, thus making the play a perfect example for illustration of this kind of comedy in English. The argument is as follows:

Wellborn, having wasted his possessions in prodigal living, casts about him for a way to recover himself. His estates have been forfeited to a rich and unscrupulous uncle, Sir Giles Overreach. Wellborn turns for help to Lady Allworth, a rich widow to whose husband he had once done a service, and out of gratitude she agrees to pretend that she is betrothed to him. The news spreads, Wellborn's credit is restored, and Sir Giles hastens to press money upon him in order to further the match, hoping through his nephew's prodigality to get possession of Lady A.'s wealth as he had already done of Wellborn's. Wellborn uses his uncle's money to pay off all his creditors.

Sir Giles has a daughter, Margaret, whom he wishes to marry to a lord. He makes overtures to Lord Lovell, who is not anxious for such an alliance, but pretends to favor it, and takes advantage of his relations thus established to plan the elopement of Margaret with young Allworth, who is in love with her.

When both the plots are ripe, the disclosures are made. Sir Giles discovers that he has lost his daughter, squandered his money on

---

[1] Cf. Vernon Lee: *Studies of the Eighteenth Century in Italy.*

false representations, and, to crown all, that the bond by which he held Wellborn's estates is not valid. Under the combined force of these blows, Sir Giles goes mad.

Here is practical joking carried to an extreme, but the harshness of the conclusion ought not to be taken too seriously, save as an indication of the state of the comic sense in Massinger's time. Madness appears to have been considered comic,[1] and even if this had not been so, a case like this is only an extreme outcome of the theory which accepts as comic the victimizing of one person by another. In this play, indeed, Sir Giles is portrayed as an arrant rascal, and his punishment represented as deserved, but it is hard for the reader to see wherein his nephew was much better. But the comedian does not always feel bound so to justify his victim's fate, and we have already seen that the "moral" Jonson with entire serenity let his honest men be outwitted and abused.

The play is typical because with two underlying serious motives it places the emphasis on the intrigue of one set of persons to outwit another. In this case there are a number of conspirators all uniting to trick one victim, whereas in Jonson the victims are usually many, the conspirators few. But the plan of movement is the same; the schemes are carried steadily forward, the victim offers no opposition worthy the name, the play has no central climax, but pushes forward evenly to the last act, which serves merely to disclose what has been previously accomplished.

Turning now to Jonson's plots, we shall find that, compared with those of Terence, or with this play of Massinger, the emphasis is less on the serious motive, and greater on the schemes for trickery. We shall find, too, much greater complexity, and often no single line of action as clearly dominant as is that of the Wellborn-Allworth plot in Massinger's play.

---

[1] Cf. John Corbin: *The Elizabethan Hamlet.*

In considering Jonson's plots it has seemed best to subject a few to careful analysis, and give others a brief treatment. Those selected, as best showing the varieties of comic structure, are *Every Man in His Humour*, *Every Man out of His Humour*, *The Alchemist*, and *Volpone*.

2. Structural Features of *Every Man in His Humour*.

The grouping of the *dramatis personae* into intriguers and victims has been alluded to. In this play the principal characters fall into the following groups:

Intriguers.
- *Young Knowell.*
- *Brainworm*, his servant.
- *Wellbred*, his friend.
- *Bridget*, Wellbred's sister-in-law, sister of Kitely. She is rather passively in league with the intriguers.

Victims who are intimately connected with the main plot.
- *Knowell*, father of young Knowell.
- *Kitely*, a merchant; his "humour" is jealousy.
- *Dame Kitely*, his wife, sister of Wellbred.
- *Downright*, half-brother of Wellbred; his "humour" is rashness and violence.

Victims whose importance is chiefly episodic.
- *Bobadill*, a captain; his "humour" is boastfulness.
- *Master Stephen*, cousin of young Knowell; his "humour" is general foolishness and a desire to ape fine airs and dashing manners.
- *Master Mathew*, friend of Bobadill and follower of Bridget; he composes verses.
- *Formal*, Clerk of Justice Clement.

Justice Clement presides over the final clearing up of misunderstandings.

the affairs of the prince, and draws down upon himself a punishment which indirectly involves his daughter as well and thus reacts on the prince. Thus, Polonius must be considered as one of the important characters in *Hamlet*, whereas Osric, for example is an episodic humor-study.

In *Every Man in His Humour* there is not so marked a central interest by which to test the values of the persons, and it is much more difficult to draw boundary lines. One might almost say that *all* the persons of the drama are episodic. There are, however, differences. Kitely is in rather close relations with the other characters, and his "humour" of jealousy is worked upon by the two young men when, for the furtherance of their schemes, they want to get him conveniently out of the way. Dame Kitely is important as a necessary corollary to Kitely, and Downright falls naturally with this group, though he might be cut out of the play without making many changes. That Bobadill is episodic will be easily seen if we contrast him with Pyrgopolinices, in Plautus' *Miles Gloriosus*. Both are braggart captains, but in the Roman play the character is made the centre of the dramatic situation. His characteristics are in part the cause of the early complication, and they are made the key to the final resolution. Bobadill's portrait is as clearly drawn as that of Pyrgopolinices, but the only thing he does besides talk is once to beat a water-carrier, and once to insult a better man than himself and get a beating in his turn.[1]

Master Stephen and Master Mathew are evidently in the play as comic filling. They are of the same breed as Master Clove and Master Orange in *Every Man out of His Humour*, and the author's comment on these last may be illuminating in this connection. They are two foolish youths who appear in but one scene, a scene laid in

---

[1] Did Aristotle have some such case in mind when he said that tragedy ought to imitate not men but action and life, and that the end of life was a mode of action not a quality? Cf. *Poetics*, VI.

the middle aisle of St. Paul's, formerly the assembling place for a motley crew of rogues and oddities. Jonson has, moreover, furnished his play with two spectators, Mitis and Cordatus, who watch its action, and speak for the author in explaining and defending it. As Clove and Orange enter, Mitis asks his companion: "What be these two, signior?" Cordatus responds: "Marry, a couple, sir, that are mere strangers to the whole scope of our play; only come to walk a turn or two in this scene of Paul's by chance."[1] Clove and Orange are an extreme case, but extreme cases are apt to be highly instructive, and this one illustrates the tendency of such comic treatment. Stephen and Mathew appear in more scenes than do Clove and Orange, but of them also we may say that "they have come to walk a turn or two .... by chance," and the difference between them and the other couple is quantitative rather than qualitative.

The subjoined analysis of the play is in one respect not so convincing as it ought to be, because while it indicates the presence of episodic humor-study in the scenes, it does not show the proportional bulk of it. No analysis can show this, for it is impossible to count the lines in a scene and say, so many lines are devoted to this, so many to that; for Jonson was too great a writer to divide his work into blocks thus, and all any diagram can do is to suggest but not fix proportions. But a single reading of the play, or of one act, will suffice to supply the necessary correction of the diagrammatic representation. As a rough indication, however, of proportional bulk, it is certainly a fair estimate of, for example, the third act, to place the amount devoted to pure humor-study at seven-eighths of the entire act. In the following analysis, those parts of each scene which are devoted to episodic humor-study are set off by brackets.[2]

---
[1] *Every Man out of His Humour*, Act III, Sc. 1; Works, II, 89.

[2] In the diagram no parts of the play have been counted as episodic humor-study except such as cannot by any stretch be construed as assisting the main action.

Act I.

Sc. 1. Street before Knowell's House.
The mistaken delivery of young Knowell's letter initiates the plot.
{ Master Stephen talks with Knowell and with the messenger.

Sc. 2. Room in Knowell's House.
Young Knowell finally gets the letter, hears that his father has seen it, and sets out for town.
{ Master Stephen talks to him and Brainworm.

Sc. 3. Lane before Cob's House.
{ Conversation between Master Mathew and Cob.

Sc. 4. Room in Cob's House.
{ Bobadill and Mathew discuss fencing and verse-making.

Act II.

Sc. 1. Hall in Kitely's House.
Kitely complains to Downright of Wellbred's wild ways.
Mathew and Bobadill enter. Bobadill insults Downright.
Kitely begins to show his "humour" of jealousy.

Sc. 2. Moorfields.
{ Brainworm, disguised as a soldier, "gulls" Master Stephen in selling him a rapier.

Sc. 3. Another part of Moorfields.
{ Knowell, on his way to town to overtake his son, discourses on the bringing up of youth. He meets Brainworm in his soldier's disguise, and takes him into service.

Act III.

Sc. 1. Room in the Windmill Tavern.
{ Young Knowell, with Stephen, meets Wellbred, with Mathew and Bobadill. Elaborate humor-study.
Brainworm joins them and discloses his trick upon Knowell.

Sc. 2. Kitely's warehouse.
  Kitely and Cash converse. Elaborate development of Kitely's "humour" of jealousy.
  { Conversation between Cob and Cash.
  { Wellbred and Young Knowell, with their three victims, converse.
  { Cob is beaten by Bobadill.
Sc. 3. Room in Justice Clement's House.
  Kitely hears that his house is full of visitors. His jealousy aroused, he rushes home.
  Cob gets a warrant to arrest Bobadill for assault.

Act IV.

Sc. 1. Room in Kitely's House.
  { Wellbred and young Knowell show off their victims for the benefit of the two ladies, Dame Kitely and Bridget.
  { Downright enters, fights with Wellbred.
  Kitely enters and drives the young men out.
  (During the scene young Knowell is supposed to fall in love with Bridget, but the only indication of this is his own statement in a later scene.)
Sc. 2. Before Cob's House.
  { Comic conversation between Cob and Tib.
Sc. 3. Room in Windmill Tavern.
  Young Knowell confesses to Wellbred his love for Bridget. Wellbred promises to compass the marriage.
Sc. 4. The Old Jewry.
  Brainworm sends Knowell to Cob's House on a fruitless chase to find his son.
  { Brainworm goes off with Formal, planning to cozen him.
Sc. 5. Moorfields.
  { Young Knowell with the three victims. Bobadill boasts his prowess in sword-play. Downright enters and beats him. Downright drops his cloak, which Stephen appropriates.

Sc. 6. Room in Kitely's House.
　Kitely's jealousy is portrayed.
　Wellbred sends Brainworm to tell Young Knowell to meet him and Bridget at the Tower.
　Wellbred sends Dame Kitely on a false errand to Cob's House. He does the same to Kitely.
　He goes off with Bridget to meet Young Knowell.

Sc. 7. A street.
　Mathew and Bobadill meet Brainworm (disguised as Formal) and ask him to arrest Downright for assault. He agrees, but forces them to pay him well for the service.

Sc. 8. Lane before Cob's House.
　Knowell, Dame Kitely and Kitely encounter one another. Mutual recriminations ensue, in which Cob and Tib are involved. They agree to refer the matter to Justice Clement.

Sc. 9. A street.
　Brainworm, in another disguise, arrests Downright for assault, and arrests Stephen for stealing Downright's cloak.

Act V.

Sc. 1. Hall in Justice Clement's House.
　Complete resolution of all misunderstandings. Brainworm is pardoned for his offenses because of their wit.

A few general comments on the play are in place here. With regard to the "unities," it will be noted that the action takes place in a single day, and is confined to the city of London and its environs, though within these limits the place is shifted with a kaleidoscopic vivacity that would have dazed Plautus or Terence. Unity of action can scarcely be said to exist: the play's only claim to unity must be based on its preservation of a uniform tone in the comic element, and its centralization of the various comic episodes in the small group of arch-conspirators who direct the entire action. Like all comedy of this type, the play can not properly be said to have any central climax or turning-point, any opposing force, any so-called "return-action." It consists so far as its plot is concerned, of a series of complications intentionally brought about by a few of the persons, and a final and comprehensive resolution brought about partly by intention and partly by chance. The play is, moreover, like Massinger's *A New Way to Pay Old Debts*, Middleton's *A Trick to Catch the Old One*, and others of this class in that this resolution is the sole business of the fifth act; up to the very end of the fourth act the complications and perplexities continue to increase.

It is noteworthy, moreover, that though Young Knowell's love for Bridget is a main motive in the latter part of the action, no space is given to the exposition of this motive. He must be supposed to fall in love with her during the first scene of Act IV, but there is not a line in the scene to show this. We are informed of it in scene 3 of the same act in the following lines:

> *Wellbred.* But, tell me ingenuously, dost thou affect my sister Bridget as thou pretend'st?
> *Young Knowell.* Friend, am I worth belief?
> *Wellbred.* Come, do not protest.

Thereupon they discuss ways and means of compassing the marriage. Wellbred and Bridget are not again on the stage together until they appear in the general assembling at Justice Clement's. This illustrates perfectly the difference between Jonson's methods and those of other comedians. If Terence had handled the same story, his treatment would have emphasized the love-motive in little scenes scattered through the play; if Shakespeare had been the author, he would have raised the love-motive to the dignity of a genuine main-plot, and without eliminating the comic incidents would have made them distinctly subordinate. Compare, with this point in view, the treatment of Dame Pliant in *The Alchemist*,[1] and, for contrast, that of Celia in *Volpone*.[2]

3. Structural Features of *Every Man out of His Humour*.

By its very title, the play confessedly aims, first to portray each person's eccentricity, and then to bring the person to discomfiture. The two agents in bringing this about are Carlo Buffone, described as " a public, scurrilous and prophane jester," and Macilente whose " humour" is envy.

The argument of the play is so disconnected that it can hardly be given as a single story. Each person has separate adventures, and the chief ground of unity is that they all know each other. The argument can therefore most conveniently be given under the heads of the different persons.

Puntarvolo, is an eccentric knight of Quixotic manners. He plans to journey to Constantinople, and puts up money on his safe return with his wife, cat and dog. If he fails, the person who has accepted his money keeps it; if he succeeds the person returns him five for one. First, his wife refuses to go, then Macilente poisons the dog. His plans are thus quashed.

Fastidious Brisk, is an affected, vain courtier, who dons a a new suit every few hours. He boasts of the favors he receives of great court ladies, especially Saviolina. Macilente first looks on while Saviolina snubs him, and then persuades Deliro to imprison him for debt.

---

[1] Cf. infra, pp. 60-4.
[2] Cf. infra, pp. 63-71.

Fungoso, is a law-student, only desirous of aping Brisk in his manners and his clothes. He is, however, always "a suit behind," and finally sees the folly of his ways.

Deliro, a citizen, foolishly indulgent to his wife. Through Macilente's agency he discovers her faithlessness and is cured of his infatuation.

Fallace, his wife, is thoroughly spoiled by his attentions. She is secretly in love with Brisk, and goes to help him in prison, but on being discovered there by her husband she is mortified into meekness.

Sordido, a wealthy and covetous farmer, melancholy at others' prosperity, hangs himself. Some peasants cut him down in time, then, seeing who he is, bewail their act. At this Sordido realizes his own evil character and repents.

Sogliardo, his brother, a clownish countryman, anxious to buy the name and manners of a gentleman. He engages Shift, a worthless impostor, to teach him to "take tobacco." He greatly admires Shift, but finally discovers that he has been duped.

Shift, "a thread-bare shark." He boasts of his bravery, but is forced by Puntarvolo to confess that he is a coward.

Saviolina, a court lady, vain of her penetration. Brisk and others introduce her to Sogliardo, telling her that he is a gentleman who amuses himself by pretending to play the clown. She vows she can detect the gentleman beneath the acting, and when she has committed herself, they discover to her her mistake.

Clove and
Orange, } two foolish "coxcombs," "twins of foppery," having no part in the action.

Mitis and
Cordatus, } are spectators of the play.

Macilente, is the person through whom all the mishaps to the others occur, except the adventure of Sordido.

Structural Features of Jonson's Satiric Comedy. 57

His chief assistant is *Carlo Buffone*, who throughout the play joins him in ridiculing the rest. Finally Macilente eggs him on to taunt Puntarvolo about the loss of his dog, and at the same time urges Puntarvolo to resent these insults, until finally the knight, roused to fury, seals up Carlo's mouth with wax.

Macilente's malice, having nothing further to feed on, becomes quiet.

The play is a remarkable illustration of the extent to which the dramatic purpose may influence the dramatic structure. As a play it is poor, but as an extreme instance of a tendency it is one of the most interesting of Jonson's productions. For Jonson's plots have such a bewildering surface complexity that it is hard to realize how simple is their underlying plan, but once the plan is perceived the complexity ceases to bewilder. Of this plan the play in question is an absolutely diagrammatic instance. The writer has started with his set of eccentric people, he has planned for each one a little plot that will first show him off and then break up his characteristic habit of mind. He then merely shuffles the persons a little, so that the treatment of any one of them shall not fall all in one place, and the plan is complete. That this is not an exaggerated statement will appear from the following summary of scenes. The summary is also made to illustrate what has already been said as to Jonson's habit of supplying his action with running commentary from the lips of some one or more of the persons in the scene. In the analysis below, the names in the margin beside each scene indicate the persons to whom this function of critic and expounder is entrusted,[1] while the names in italics indicate the persons whose "humours" form the basis of the action.

---

[1] On this point, cf. the remarks on *Cynthia's Revels*, infra, pp. 82-3.

Act I.

Macilente and Carlo.	Sc. 1. *Macilente* betrays his "humour" of envy. *Sogliardo*, encouraged by Carlo, expresses his intention of becoming a gentleman. *Sordido*, plans to hoard his grain till time of famine, to sell high.

Act II.

Chiefly Carlo.	Sc. 1. *Fastidious Brisk* and *Sogliardo* exhibit their characteristic "humours." *Puntarvolo* exhibits his eccentricities of manner, and proposes his plan for travel. *Fungoso* admires Brisk's suit and plans to copy it.
Macilente.	Sc. 2. *Deliro* and *Fallace* are portrayed, Deliro anxiously attentive, Fallace indifferent or querulous. *Fungoso* appears in a suit copied from Brisk's.

Act III.

Mitis and Cordatus.	Sc. 1. *Clove* and *Orange* converse.
Carlo and Macilente.	*Brisk, Deliro, Puntarvolo, Carlo, Sogliardo*, and *Macilente*, indulge in characteristic conversation. *Fungoso* brings a tailor to copy Brisk's new suit. *Shift* is engaged to instruct *Sogliardo* in taking tobacco.
Mitis and Cordatus.	Sc. 2. *Sordido* hangs himself, is cut down, and is seized with remorse.
Macilente.	Sc. 3. *Brisk* visits Saviolina at court. He is snubbed, and Macilente witnesses his discomfiture.

Act. IV.

Sc. 1. *Fungoso* and *Fallace* are further portrayed. Deliro resolves to press Brisk for his debts.

Sc. 2. *Fallace* sends Fungoso to warn Brisk.

Sc. 3. *Macilente* tries to arouse Deliro's jealousy, and fails.

Carlo, Puntarvolo, and Macilente.

Sc. 4. *Puntarvolo* completes his plans for travel.

Macilente describes *Brisk's* rebuff at court.

Sogliardo, Shift, and *Brisk* carry on characteristic conversation.

Sc. 5. *Fungoso*, in another new suit.

Macilente.

Sc. 6. Macilente proposes to the others a plan to bring *Saviolina* "out of her humour" of self-conceit. General conversation.

Fungoso enters, finds Brisk in yet another suit, and swoons.

Act. V.

Sc. 1. Macilente poisons *Sogliardo's* dog.

The whole company unite in criticism of the victim.

Sc. 2. *Saviolina* is brought "out of her humour."

Sc. 3. *Puntarvolo* misses his dog. Macilente accuses *Shift* of stealing it. Shift is terrorized into retracting his former boasts, and slinks away in disgrace

Macilente.

Sogliardo is down-cast at the exposure of his friend.

Macilente.

Sc. 4. *Carlo* taunts Puntarvolo, who seals his lips with wax.

Carlo and *Brisk* are arrested.

Macilente.

Sc. 5. Macilente gets *Fallace* to visit Brisk in prison.

Sc. 6. *Fungoso* repents of his follies. *Deliro* is incited by Macilente to bring an action for debt against *Brisk*.

Macilente.

Sc. 7. *Fallace*, visiting Brisk in prison makes love to him. She is surprised by Deliro and Macilente. Macilente's envy is appeased.

4. Structural Features of *The Alchemist*.

In *The Alchemist* the relations between the victims and the victimizers are not quite so simple as in the two plays just treated. Hence the grouping here given holds good for the first part of the play, but needs modification for the latter part, as will appear in the detailed discussion.

Intriguers.
- *Face*, steward of Lovewit's House. "Captain Face" is his assumed name.
- *Subtle*, the Alchemist, pretending to power in all the occult sciences.
- *Dol Common*, a courtezan, their colleague.

Victims.
- *Dapper*, a lawyer's clerk.
- *Drugger*, a youth who has just set up a drug and tobacco shop.
- *Sir Epicure Mammon*, a wealthy Knight, whose characteristics are greed of wealth and proneness to every form of sensual indulgence.
- *Tribulation Wholesome*, *Ananias*, } Puritan Elders.
- *Kastril*, a young heir, come to town to learn the arts of swaggering and quarreling.
- *Dame Pliant*, his sister, a widow.

Surly, a friend of Mammon, who suspects the Alchemist of fraud.

Lovewit, owner of the house, by whom the resolution is occasioned.

Structural Features of Jonson's Satiric Comedy. 61

ARGUMENT.—In the absence of Lovewit, his steward, under the name of Captain Face, invites Subtle and Dol Common to set up business in the empty house. They do so, and on various pretenses extort money from various customers. To Sir Epicure Mammon, Subtle promises the philosopher's stone, and Mammon brings loads of iron pots, tin pans, etc., to be turned into gold. Subtle has held out the same hopes to the Puritan Elders, and he sells to them Mammon's metal vessels, representing them to be "orphans' goods" and guaranteeing to turn them into gold when the process of making the stone shall have been consummated. Dapper and Drugger are less important victims, but young Kastril and his widow sister are valuable because Dame Pliant is a desirable matrimonial candidate. Face and Subtle quarrel for her, but Subtle gives way. He assures the widow that she is to marry a Spaniard, and they privately send Drugger for a Spanish costume, assuring him that he shall have her.

Meanwhile Surly, who suspects the whole establishment, enters, disguised as a Spaniard. The ruse works, and Subtle and Face talk freely before him, thus betraying themselves. Surly discloses to Dame Pliant her dangerous position, and in return asks her hand in marriage. Face temporarily meets the crisis by setting Kastril, Drugger and Ananias on Surly, and they, ignorant of the real situation, beat him out of doors.

At this juncture Lovewit, master of the house, is heard outside, demanding admittance. He is beset by neighbors, who relate the strange doings there have been during his absence. Face, having shaved and resumed his steward's garb, comes out and tries to pacify Lovewit and get him away. While they are talking Surly returns bringing Mammon, now undeceived, and officers to arrest the scoundrels. The Puritan Elders also appear with officers, and finally there are heard from within the cries of Dapper, who has been shut up to get him out of the way. Face, seeing the hopelessness of his case, confesses everything to his master, and promises him all their spoils, besides the widow, if he will pardon the abuse of his house. Lovewit agrees, and Face re-enters the house, gets possession of the trunks of valuables and then commands Subtle and Dol to leave at once if they want to escape arrest. They accuse him of treachery, but there is no redress and they are forced to precipitate flight. Face invests Lovewit with the Spanish costume Drugger has brought and marries him to the widow.

Surly finds no one to arrest, and discovers that the widow, too, has slipped through his hands.

This play, like the preceding one, presents merely a series of trickeries. But it differs in the management of the latter part, where the conspirators are met with rather formidable opposition, headed by Surly and reinforced by some of the victims who begin to apprehend the cheat. Thus, whereas the first three acts progress quietly enough, the fourth and fifth involve radical changes in the relations of the persons. The grouping in the first three acts may be thus simply represented:

Act I. $\left.\begin{array}{l}\textit{Face}\\ \textit{Subtle}\\ \textit{Dol}\end{array}\right\}$ dupe $\left\{\begin{array}{l}\textit{Dapper}\\ \textit{Drugger}\end{array}\right.$

Act. II. $\left.\begin{array}{l}\textit{Face}\\ \textit{Subtle}\\ \textit{Dol}\end{array}\right\}$ dupe $\left\{\begin{array}{l}\textit{Mammon}\\ \textit{Ananias}\\ \textit{Drugger}\end{array}\right.$

Act III. $\left.\begin{array}{l}\textit{Face}\\ \textit{Subtle}\\ \textit{Dol}\end{array}\right\}$ dupe $\left\{\begin{array}{l}\textit{Ananias}\\ \textit{Tribulation Wholesome}\\ \textit{Kastril}\\ \textit{Dapper}\end{array}\right.$

Act IV. starts out in the usual way, first with Mammon as the dupe, and then with Kastril and Dame Pliant. The duping of Mammon and of Kastril continues throughout the act, but the entrance of Surly, at the end of Scene 1, in his Spanish disguise, introduces an element of opposition. For a time relations are reversed, and the intriguers are distinctly at a disadvantage. In Scene 2, Surly is presented to Dame Pliant. Scene 3 carries forward the trick on Mammon, but in Scene 4 Surly re-enters with the widow, having revealed to her his identity and warned her of her danger. Things look black for the intriguers, but when Surly throws off his disguise and threatens them with exposure Face meets the emergency by setting on the intruder two of the other dupes, Kastril and Drugger, while Ananias joins in abusing him on religious grounds connected with his "idolatrous" Spanish costume, and their combined attack forces Surly out of the house.

At this moment a new element of opposition arises, in the arrival of Lovewit, which ends the act.

Structural Features of Jonson's Satiric Comedy.

The grouping in the act, is, then, as follows:

Beginning of Scene 1.	*Face* *Subtle* *Dol* }	dupe	{ *Mammon* *Kastril* *Dame Pliant*
End of Scene 1.	*Surly*	dupes	{ *Face* *Subtle*
Scene 2.	"	"	"
Scene 3.	*Face* *Subtle* *Dol* }	dupe	*Mammon*
Scene 4.	*Surly* *Dame Pliant* }	in open conflict with	{ *Face* *Subtle* } assisted by { *Kastril* *Drugger* *Ananias*

In other words, there occurs first a reversal of relations—the dupers become dupes—and finally an open conflict of forces in which Surly is worsted.

In Act V. there are further modifications. The intriguers are first menaced by Lovewit's presence, then Surly's return with Mammon and the officers adds to the danger. The other dupes enter, and failing to get admission they too take alarm and set out to get officers. Finally, Dapper's muffled cries precipitate the crisis.

Up to this point the grouping has been:

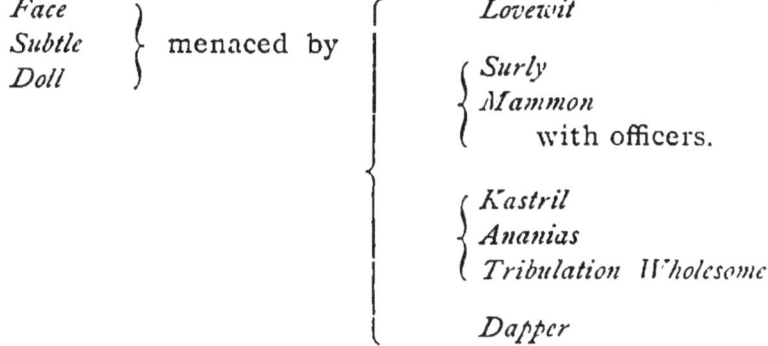

Face *Subtle* *Doll* } menaced by { *Lovewit* ; { *Surly* *Mammon* with officers. ; { *Kastril* *Ananias* *Tribulation Wholesome* ; *Dapper*

At this point Face, to save himself, breaks away from the other two, joins forces with Lovewit, brings Dame Pliant and Kastril to his side through the marriage, and is thus strong enough to face the remaining opposition. The new and final grouping is:

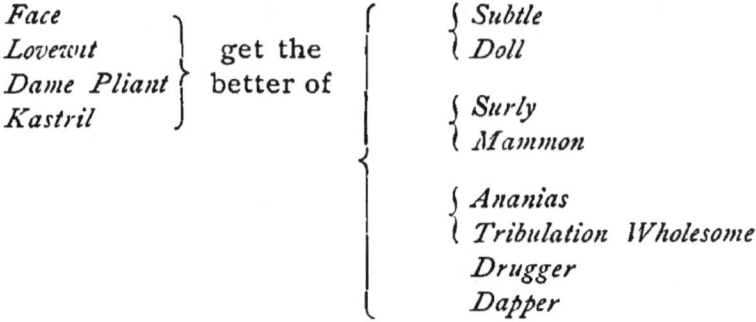

The play thus resembles *Every Man in His Humour* in that its basis is a series of tricks and impostures. It differs in that the relations between the persons are not constant, but undergo two rather radical alterations, the last one amounting to a complete reconstruction. In some ways the conclusion is like that of the earlier play. Lovewit, like Justice Clement, comes in from outside to preside over the resolution, and he pardons Face as Clement does Brainworm, " for the wit of the offence," though Lovewit has the added motive that the servant's offence has been most profitable to the master.

There are, however, more interesting points of likeness with *Volpone*, which will be discussed under the latter play.

5. Structural Feature of *Volpone*.

There is a distinct sub-interest in this play, that of Sir Politick Would-be, which necessitates two sets of groups.

For the main play:

Chief intriguers.
- *Volpone*, an old and wealthy Venetian noble.
- *Mosca*, his parasite.

Chief victims.
- *Voltore*, an advocate.
- *Corvino*, a merchant.
- *Corbaccio*, a feeble old gentleman.
- *Lady Politick Would-be*, wife of Sir Politick.

All are legacy-hunters who beset Volpone.

Temporarily victims, but ultimately agents of the opposition.
- *Bonario*, son of Corbaccio.
- *Celia*, wife of Corvino.

For the sub-interest:

Peregrine, an Englishman, who ridicules and finally exposed Sir Politick's folly.

Sir Politick Would-be, an Englishman who pretends to be keen in matters of politics and finance.

ARGUMENT OF THE MAIN PLOT.—Volpone, being beset by legacy-hunters, gets both amusement and wealth out of their attentions. He pretends to be at the point of death, and Mosca, his fertile-brained parasite, persuades each visitor in turn that he has hopes of being the heir, provided he continue showering attentions on the dying man. They therefore present Volpone with rich jewels, but scarely try to hide their eagerness for his death. Hearing of the beautiful wife of Corvino, one of these legacy-hunters, Volpone desires possession of her, and in the disguise of a mountebank doctor he succeeds in getting a glimpse of her at her window. Mosca goes to Corvino and tells him that Volpone is very feeble and that the physicians say that there is but one means to prolong his life, and this is that some young woman be procured to sleep by him and lend him vigor. Corvino is finally wrought upon to offer his wife, on Mosca's representation that this act will surely secure to him the inheritance. Mosca, meeting Bonario, tells him, what is in fact the truth, that his father, Corbaccio, has disinherited him, and made Volpone his heir, in hopes that Volpone will reciprocate. Bonario, distrustful, goes to Volpone's house to assure himself. While he is there Corvino comes, forcing in Celia. He leaves her with Volpone, who, throwing off his disguise of sick man, first woos her and then tries to force her. Hearing her cries, Bonario rushes in, rescues her, and leaves the house vowing to punish such crime through the law courts.

Mosca meets the danger by enlisting in his service all the legacy-hunters. Corvino's evident interest lies in facing down Celia's accusations. Corbaccio's also lies in opposing the son he has disinherited, while the lawyer Voltore, not knowing all the facts, is glad to plead the cause of his patron. Mosca cleverly avoids arousing the jealousy of his assistants toward one another, and the trial goes against Bonario and Celia, the culminating point being when Volpone, apparently dying, is carried into court on a litter.

Elated with such success, Volpone determines to give out that he has died and left Mosca sole heir. This is done, and the eager legacy-hunters, hurrying to the house to see the will, find Mosca, richly dressed, taking account of his possessions. Not content with watching their discomfiture, Volpone pursues them in disguise, taunting them with their disappointment. At last, harassed and enraged, Voltore retracts the evidence he had given in court, thus exposing Mosca, Corbaccio and Corvino. Volpone, still in his disguise, listens with alarm, and whispers to Voltore that Volpone yet lives and has made him heir. Voltore thereupon returns to his first testimony.

Meanwhile Mosca has determined to keep in earnest what his patron had given him in jest. He enters court and affirms Volpone's death, while the disguised Volpone asserts that he lives. Furious at his parasite's treachery, Volpone at last throws off his disguise; the whole matter is explained; Bonario and Celia are cleared and reparation is made them; Mosca is sent to the galleys, Volpone to prison for life; to the others is meted out appropriate punishment.

This complicated plot has some striking points of correspondence with that of *The Alchemist*, and some with that of the tragedy, *Sejanus*.

The schemes of the main action originate in two vicious characters acting together and imposing on others, getting out of their cozening both amusement and profit. They ridicule their victims as Face, Subtle and Dol do theirs, and the victims themselves are, as in *The*

Alchemist, for the most part scoundrels who scarcely deserve pity. Dame Pliant, in *The Alchemist*, was an innocent if very foolish victim, but her counterpart Celia, in *Volpone*, is a really pathetic figure. Her rescue by Bonario may be paralled with the attempted rescue of Dame Pliant by Surly and it will be remembered that in meeting Surly's aggression Face called in some of his dupes—Kastril, Drugger and Ananias—to his assistance, just as Mosca here calls in Voltore and the rest. There are important differences between the two incidents, which will be reverted to later. Finally, the Volpone-Mosca league like that of Face, Subtle and Dol, is threatened by a "turning of the worm" on the part of their dupes, and the league itself is finally broken, Mosca deserting his patron as Face deserted Subtle and Dol, though he does not escape punishment as Face did.

As in *The Alchemist*, the grouping in the early part of the play is simple enough, the persons falling into the two lists of dupers and duped, but later on the opposition arises; dupers and dupe coalesce for the moment; then the group disintegrates and the final resolution occurs. The beginning of the change, however, occurs in the third act of *Volpone*, instead of the fourth, giving the play more nearly the usual form of a tragedy, whose turning-point commonly falls in the third act.

The grouping in the acts is here given, for convenience of comparison with *The Alchemist*.

Act	Dupers		Duped
Act I.	*Volpone* *Mosca*	dupe	*Voltore* *Corbaccio* *Corvino*
Act II.	*Volpone* *Mosca*	dupe	*Corvino*
Act III.	*Volpone* *Mosca*	dupe	*Lady-Would-be*
but later,	*Bonario* *Celia*	raise an opposition to	*Volpone* *Mosca*

as a result, *Mosca* affiliates with the legacy-hunters, and an open conflict follows, grouped thus:

Act IV. $\left.\begin{array}{l}Bonario\\Celia\end{array}\right\}$ versus $\left\{\begin{array}{l}Mosca\\Volpone\\Voltore\\Corbaccio\\Corvino\\Lady\ Would\text{-}be.\end{array}\right.$

Act V. The alliance is severed, and the grouping again becomes:

$\left.\begin{array}{l}Volpone\\Mosca\end{array}\right\}$ duping $\left\{\begin{array}{l}Voltore\\Corbaccio\\Corvino\\Lady\ Would\text{-}be\end{array}\right.$

finally, *Voltore* joins the opposition, *Mosca* breaks with *Volpone*, and retribution overtakes alike dupers and duped.

Before completing the discussion of the play, it is necessary to say a few words as to the usual requisites of a comedy. Comedy, as we have seen, finds its material wherever there is a departure from a recognized norm. The basis of judgment may be moral, as in Molière's *Tartuffe,* or social, as in his *Le Misanthrope.* The first play assumes a norm of society based on honesty and fair-dealing; the vicious hypocrite is the exception and therefore the comic butt. The second assumes a norm of society based on convention, deceit and jealousy; the honest man is the exception and therefore the comic butt. Similarly, *The Alchemist* is scaled for a world of witty rogues, and the one honest man in it, Surly, meets nothing but discomfiture, while the various rascals fare ill or well according to luck and their own brains. For the purposes of the comedian either assumption will serve—of a world of rogues or of honest men—provided only he carries us with him, makes us accept his position, at least temporarily.[1] In *Le Misanthrope* Molière scarcely does this, inasmuch as we are inclined to sympathize with the comic butt, Alceste, instead of with the conventional society which rejects him. It is a sign of Jonson's success in preserving whatever tone he has taken, that his plays have been accepted without question as "moral," despite their frequent contravening or ignoring of moral laws. In *The Alchemist* more particularly, the necessary tone is preserved without a break. The intriguers of the play do actually, it is true, commit crimes, but their victims are criminal too, in intent if not in performance, and, thus left to choose between brilliant rascals and foolish ones, we side with the first. Dame Pliant's relations might, indeed, have been too serious for comedy, but they are not allowed to become so, and her final marriage is treated as lightly as the rest, it takes place off the stage, and, in fact, she herself appears in only three scenes and in these her lines are few and unimportant. Finally, Surly, an honest man, fares rather badly, but he is so treated as not to arouse very keen sympathy. His sneering tone is not attractive, and his discomfiture is not so serious as to claim our pity. He has merely interfered in other people's affairs, and, save for a little abusive language and a few knocks, he comes out with neither gain nor loss.

Returning to *Volpone*, we note the contrast. As the play starts out, we are in a world of scoundrels again, but they are grimmer and their vices are more revolting than those in *The Alchemist*. Perhaps the fact that here they are almost all old men makes part of the difference; perhaps a part is due to the difference in the kind of victimizing. For the active, agile roguery of Subtle and Face is at least enlivening, but there is something almost oppressive in the way Volpone lies back and lets vice expose itself before his gaze, while he enjoys the spectacle as a devil might enjoy watching sin.

---

[1] This is the basis of truth in the paradoxes of Lamb's essay *On The Artificial Comedy of the Last Century*, though one can hardly accept all his conclusions.

Furthermore, with the introduction of the Celia episodes whatever comic tone still remained is broken through. Uniting as they do what is revolting in motive with what is beautiful—almost gorgeous—in language, they introduce into the play an element which trenches on the tragic. Celia is not like Dame Pliant, Bonario is not like Surly. Both are high spirited, pure-minded, and the spectacle of Celia facing first her husband and then Volpone, the court-room scene where she and her champion are crushed beneath what appears a damning weight of evidence—these are not scenes for comedy. The fact that there is actually no tragic calamity—that "no one slays or is slain"—and that Celia and Bonario are finally released by the court with apologies and an attempt at reparation, in no way compensates for what has gone before; the ground-tone of comedy, the comic color-scale, if one may use a figure, has been broken through.

It may have been a sense of this that led Jonson to insert the episodes of Sir Politick Would-be, but if these are the result of an attempt to restore the comic balance the attempt was unfortunate. The vapid harangues of the fatuous but harmless gentlemen neither harmonize with the grim irony of the rest of the play nor do they furnish agreeable relief.

In his management of the final resolution the author was more fortunate. The usual comic *denouement* where at least no one is hurt and every one is forgiven, was manifestly unfit, and recognizing this Jonson ventured to mete out to his persons punishment only less severe than death. That he did this deliberately, and somewhat under compulsion of the conditions he had created, we may infer from his remarks in the Dedicatory Letter, where he apologizes for his departure from traditional form.[1]

" And though my catastrophe may, in the strict rigor of comic law, meet with censure . . . . I desire the learned and charitable critic, to have so much faith in me, to think it was done of industry."[1]

---

[1] Dedication, *Volpone;* Works, III, 159.

The play is, indeed, as near tragedy as comedy, and in structure it is transitional between the two. Many of its events are of the typical comic type, but the Celia episode, falling at the end of the third act, has the force of a climax such as one usually finds in a tragedy or serious drama in about this position. It serves, moreover, as a real turning point in the action, and is the ultimate cause of the catastrophe, though the immediate cause is the separation of Mosca and Volpone. The part of the play following this incident might almost be classed as a regular "return-action" such as is almost always found in serious or tragic drama.

The resemblance between this play and *Sejanus* has been already suggested. The tone in the tragedy is only a little grimmer, as the issues involved are larger. The central characters, Sejanus and Tiberius, are different from Volpone and Mosca, but their powers of intellect and imagination are not greater, nor does the language of the tragedy ever reach greater force and splendor than that of the comedy. Moreover, their structure has points of resemblance. At the beginning of the play the two gigantic criminals, Tiberius and Sejanus, are in league. Acting together they crush one after another of their enemies. At length, however, Sejanus presumes too far, he proposes his own marriage with Drusus' widow. The distrust of Tiberius is aroused, and he determines to crush his too-powerful favorite before he is himself over-topped. The last part of the play deals with the struggle between the two, ending in the annihilation of Sejanus. The union in crime of the two men, and then their swinging asunder, their relations to their victims and to each other, appear to be a tragic counterpart of the situation in Volpone.

As an actual fact, the order in which the plays were written is the reverse of that adopted in the present treatment. The date of *Sejanus* was 1603; of *Volpone*, 1605; of *The Alchemist*, 1610. It is tempting to draw inferences based on this order, but these might be only fanciful. Thus much is, however, clear: *Volpone* is the one of Johnson's comedies least like comedy. In its tone, in its character, in its story, in its structure, it leans towards tragedy. Perhaps the best thing to do with it would be to class it with *Sejanus* and *Catiline* as ironic drama.

CHAPTER V.

JONSON'S ROMANTIC COMEDY.

That Jonson had ever written any but satiric humor-comedy is hard to realize, for we are accustomed to thinking of him as one whose powers, like those of his own humor-ridden creations, "ran all one way." And indeed, the mature Jonson is singularly unvarying in point of view and in practice. We might apply to him Aurelia's mocking reproach to her sister:

"What, true-stitch, sister! Both your sides alike!"[1]

But unvarying as he seems, Jonson had his romantic period. A few years younger than Shakespeare, he was still doing hackwork of the stage, recasting old plays, and acting, while the elder poet was producing his early comedies—*Love's Labour's Lost*, *The Comedy of Errors*, *The Two Gentlemen of Verona*, *A Midsummer Night's Dream*, and *The Merchant of Venice*. It is difficult to suppose that Jonson should have been uninfluenced by this wonderful series of plays, even if we imagine him, according to the conventional picture, with his eyes glued to the page of Plautus and Terence and Seneca. Of such influence we find few traces in his typical work and his expressed theory, but that it was for a time strong, parts of some of his plays and the whole of one give evidence.

This one is *The Case Is Altered*,[2] produced apparently at the end of 1598, a few months after *Every Man in His Humour*. So different is this from his usual work, that it has been questioned whether the play really is Jonson's. The earliest printed form known to us is a

---

[1] *The Case Is Altered*, Act II, Sc. 3; Works VI, 331.
[2] For the argument of this play cf. Appendix, pp. 95, 96.

quarto of 1609, of which some copies give Jonson's name, others do not, and we may take our choice of two hypotheses: either Jonson's name was unwarrantably inserted by the printers, and taken out of some copies by the writer's own orders; or it was printed without credit to him, and his name afterwards inserted.[1] Thus far no other evidence is forthcoming. Gifford and Cunningham both accept the play as Jonson's, as do all his critics, except C. H. Herford who, in his introduction to the 'Mermaid' edition of Jonson, writes: "The same year [1599!] probably produced a fourth [play], still extant, in which it seems equally clear that Jonson wrote a part, and that he did not write the whole—*The Case Is Altered*."[2] Mr. Herford gives no hint of his reasons either for dating the play a year later, or for denying its accepted authorship. The "part" written by Jonson is, we presume, Valentine's satirical description of the "Utopian" (English) stage, the hit at Anthony Munday, and the Jaques incident. But this last, which is unquestionably Jonson's, is so intimately bound in with the Rachel-plot that to accept it as Jonson's almost involves accepting work as unlike his usual manner as any in the play.

Assuming, then, that the play is Jonson's, we have the interesting case of a purely "Romantic" comedy written by the greatest of the opposed school. It might almost be interpolated into the series of Shakespeare's comedies just mentioned—it would certainly be no more puzzling there than is *All's Well that Ends Well* in a later group. Structurally it is far above *Love's Labour's Lost*, though it has nothing so masterly as the great exposure scene of that play. If we had to place the play we should put it about with *The Two Gentlemen of Verona*, when Shakespeare's comedy was passing out of its stage of farce and situation, into its distinctive early form.

---

[1] Cf. Fleay: *A Chronicle of the English Drama;* I, 357-358.
[2] Herford: Introduction to *The Best Plays of Ben Jonson*, p. xxv.

It may be worth while to pause a moment over these early plays. *Love's Labour's Lost* consists of one situation, the exposure of the four "forsworn" youths,—a scene worked out with a cleanness of stroke worthy of Molière. Indeed the motive of the play and its attitude strongly suggest Molière. Armado might be a study of a humor, and the catastrophe, where the four gentlemen are by the loving discipline of their ladies brought 'out of their humours' is Jonsonesque. Biron's recantation:

> Taffeta phrases, silken terms precise,
> I do forswear them, and I here protest,
> * * * * * *
> Henceforth my wooing mind shall be express'd
> In russet yeas and honest Kersey noes.[1]

finds a parallel—somewhat extravagant, indeed—in the litany of the reformed revellers in *Cynthia's Revels:*

> From Spanish shrugs, French faces, smirks, irpes,
> and all affected humors,
> Good Mercury defend us, etc.[2]

The Comedy of Errors, largely farcical, adds nothing, except perhaps a firmer grasp of the laws of structure and plot. But in *The Two Gentlemen of Verona* the note of "Romantic Comedy" is clear. The interwoven love-plots give the delicate but firm setting, while Launce with his foil and victim Speed, serve as the most good natured of burlesques on the lofty raptures of the lovers.

The likeness between this play and *The Case Is Altered* is rather interesting. In part it can be reduced to details, in part it is a case of "atmosphere," or of the writer's attitude. One of the most striking points is the fact that the humor is the same. Onion and Juniper are, to be sure, not so bright as Launce and Speed, their humor is at once less funny and more coarse—there is no surer way of appreciating Shakespeare's delicate-

---
[1] *Love's Labour's Lost*, V, 2.
[2] Palinode, *Cynthia's Revels*, V, 3; Works, III, 337, 359.

mindedness than to compare his humorous scenes with those of his contemporaries—but it is the same in kind, it is the comedy of sympathy. We laugh at Juniper, "sweet youth, whose tongue has a happy turn when he sleeps," and at Onion, the ardent lover of Rachel, but we are fond of the fellows, and our laugh is very different from that provoked by "Master Stephen," or by any of the rest of the "gulls" and fools of Jonson's world. Moreover, the use of the comic element is somewhat the same in both. In *The Two Gentlemen of Verona*, following immediately on the farewell of Julia and Proteus, comes Launce's version of his own heartrending parting from his family—depicted the more graphically with the aid of his slippers and his stony-hearted dog. Again, hard upon Valentine, steeped in "endless dolor" at his banishment from Silvia, comes Launce again with the announcement that he too is in love:—

"He lives not now that knows me to be in love; yet I am in love; but a team of horse shall not pluck that from me; nor who 'tis I love; and yet 'tis a woman; but what woman I will not tell myself; and yet 'tis a milkmaid."[1]

The parody in *The Case Is Altered* is not so consistent nor so pointed, yet we can hardly miss the kindly satire implied in Onion's wooing of Rachel, even though it is separated by a whole act from the ardent pursuit of her by the various gentlemen of rank.

Onion. O brave! she's yonder: O terrible! she's gone.

Juniper. Yea, so nimble in your dilemmas, and your hyperboles! *Hey my love! O my love!* at the first sight, by the mass.

Onion. O how she scudded! O sweet scud, how she tripped! O delicate trip and go![2]

In the serious parts of the play the intermingling of jest and earnest suggests Shakespeare. The two young

---

[1] *The Two Gentlemen of Verona*, III, 1.
[2] *The Case Is Altered*, IV, 4; Works, VI, 364.

girls, introducing themselves through Aurelia's mock-solemn announcement:

" Room for a case of matrons, colored black."

enter the scene almost like another Rosalind and Celia —at least they might have been first studies for them. Paulo, the ardent young lover, and Angelo, his faithless friend, remind us of Valentine and Proteus; indeed in V, 3 the exposure of Angelo's treachery by his friend and their instantaneous reconciliation is a situation identical with the conclusion of *The Two Gentlemen of Verona*.

Only the character of Jaques is out of keeping with the rest. He is distinctly Jonsonesque,[1] and in his addresses to his gold we feel the power of the author of *Volpone*, though even here there is a reminiscence of Shakespeare in his cry:

" Thou hast made away my child, thou hast my gold:

* * * * * * *

The thief is gone, my gold's gone, Rachel's gone."[2]

Another point is the presence of sub-plots, or at least sub-interests. It is hard to decide what we can call the principal plot, but perhaps the Camillo-Gasper interest may serve as well as any. Besides this, we have: (1) the interests centering directly about Rachel, Paulo's love and Angelo's treachery being the central issues, while the infatuation of Ferneze, of Christophero and of Onion (!) are side interests; (2) the interest centering round Jaques, his gold, and his secret; this shades into (3) the Juniper and Onion interests, while (4) Aurelia and Chamont form a very slight fourth interest. All these threads are dexterously interwoven to a loose but fairly even tissue,—too even, perhaps, for the lack of a predominating group of characters is a fault.[3]

---

[1] That he was modelled on Plautus is only another indication of this—such work was characteristic of Jonson.

[2] *The Case Is Altered*, V, 1; Works, VI, 380.

[3] Nor is the texture without flaw; the two characters, Balladino and Francisco Colonnia, are hangers-on in the play. The first was evidently inserted as a "local hit." The presence of the second seems unmotived.

Finally, it will be noted that the comic element is found not in any of the more important plots, but in the under-issues or asides. This is a trait of the "Romantic" comedy; in Jonson's typical plays, the comic element is bound up with—is contained in—the main action.

The play, then, is distinctly romantic, and if we accept it as Jonson's it acquires peculiar significance as an indication of the kind of work he might have done in this field if he had chosen it for his mature activity.[1] That it was possibly written after his first play in his later manner need not be a difficulty.[2] With a poet who worked as consciously and deliberately as Jonson it would have been quite possible to write a play in the accepted manner, even while he was in the act of breaking away from that manner.[3]

It is interesting to note that in this, his one "Romantic" comedy, Jonson follows the Roman comedians more closely than anywhere else. In the Jaques incidents the *Aulularia* was his model, in the Camillo-Gasper plot he was adapting from the *Captivi*. This would seem to bear out what was said in a preceding chapter as to the romantic possibilities of the Roman plots. The fact that Jonson so easily gave to his material the treatment needed to make these possibilities actual, is, moreover, an indication of his native power in other fields than those wherein he chose to excel. For this play, while not without faults, has in its manner a lightness of touch, in its humor a humaneness that is not equalled in the early work—scarcely in the mature work—of any contemporary save Shakespeare. That he turned aside

---

[1] *The New Inn* is sometimes called a romantic comedy, and with a degree of reason. Cf. Appendix, pp. 94, 95. On the other hand, the romantic fragment, *The Sad Shepherd*, ought to be classed with Theocritus and Spenser, as romantic pastoral, rather than with romantic comedy.

[2] Koeppel, however, thinks it was his first work. Cf. his *Quellen-Studien zu den Dramen Ben Jonson's, John Marston's und Beaumont's und Fletcher's*, pp. 1, 19.

[3] The hit at Anthony Munday, Act I, sc. 1, may, indeed, be also a comment on some of the criticism to which the new play, *Every Man in His Humour*, must certainly have given rise.

to follow other courses we must, in the case of so conscious and conscientious an artist, attribute to deliberate choice; and in making an estimate of him we ought not to ignore, as critics have sometimes done, these two of his works wherein he showed other powers than those which he ordinarily allowed free play. Lightly to set aside *The Case Is Altered* and *The Sad Shepherd* as exceptions which need not be considered "in making up the main account" is only to justify the poet's slurs on "the world's coarse thumb and finger." Exceptional they are, but not accidental or unimportant.

Perhaps Jonson was right in choosing as he did, since in the work which he made characteristically his own he had no equal, whereas in the realms that he abandoned he would have had one superior. Yet the lover of Jonson cannot but find something pathetic in this self-imposed narrowing of his mighty powers,—cannot but wish that in determining the direction of his artistic genius, in pruning its growth, he had been a little less severe, less ruthless.

APPENDIX.

BRIEF DISCUSSION OF THE COMEDIES NOT ALREADY TREATED.

CYNTHIA'S REVELS.

Of this play Gifford himself confesses that "the plot of the drama is so finely spun that no eye perhaps but Jonson's has ever been able to trace it."[1] After such an admission, from such a source, there is no need to say that the structure of the play is hardly worth comment. The story, such as it is, is as follows:

> Cynthia ordains a night of revels. In her court, though not in her immediate train, are a number of courtiers and ladies characterized by various kinds of folly.
>
> Mercury, sent by Jove, summons Echo from hiding and permits her to give expression to her grief. At the close of her lament she christens anew the fountain of Narcissus, calling it the Fountain of Self Love. Mercury and Cupid now disguise themselves as pages and enter the service of a courtier and a lady.
>
> The courtiers and ladies all drink of the Fountain of Self Love, and are even more lost in self-esteem than before. Their prime aversion is Crites, described as a perfect man, who is a member of the intimate circle of Cynthia's attendants. The courtiers revile him, but he is indifferent to their abuse. They arrange a tournament in the arts of Courtship, in which one of their number, Asotus, challenges all comers. Mercury, disguised as a Frenchman, and Crites, accept the challenge and worst their antagonists, subjecting them to merciless ridicule.
>
> In Cynthia's honor, Crites arranges a masque, wherein the courtiers and ladies, with Mercury and Cupid, take part. During the dance Cupid tries to use his arrows on some of the company, but finds that the Waters of Self Love annul the efficacy of his charms.
>
> Cynthia orders the dancers to unmask. Cupid is discovered and is censured for daring to intrude. The others are committed by Cynthia to Crites for correction. He imposes a penance, and directs them finally to drink of the well of knowledge.

There is no need of analysis. The play has no peculiar features, and is chiefly significant as showing all the faults of Jonson's method and none of the virtues. Crites, who evidently stands for Jonson, is insufferably self-righteous, and if Jonson had been more keenly

---

[1] Gifford's note to the play; Works. II, 136.

alive to the comic in himself, the character would never have been created.

Cupid and Mercury, too, act merely as critics of the other characters. One section of the play is worth calling attention to, because it is an extreme instance of Jonson's habit of portraying a character by letting someone else talk about it:—in Moulton's phrase, "alleging" character rather than "presenting" it.[1] The part in question is the whole of Act II, which may be summed up thus:

> Cupid and Mercury enter, as pages. After a few preliminary words, Mercury describes Hedon to Cupid.
>
> Hedon and Anaides (two courtiers) enter, and converse a few moments, then go off.
>
> Cupid thereupon asks Mercury who Anaides is, and Mercury describes him at length.
>
> Amorphus and Asotus (two other courtiers) enter, and converse a few moments, then go off.
>
> Cupid asks Mercury who Asotus is, and Mercury responds with a yet longer description of him.
>
> Finally "Crites passes over the stage," and Mercury launches into a warm eulogy of his perfections.

This finishes up the men. The women begin to enter, and it is Cupid's turn.

> First, "Argurion passes over the stage." Cupid describes her in full, until Mercury interrupts with, "Peace, Cupid, here comes more work for you, another character or two," and three more ladies enter, Phantaste, Moria, and Philautia.
>
> Moria utters a sentence, and Mercury asks: "Good Jove, what reverend gentlewoman in years may this be?" Cupid answers with an elaborate description, until Mercury cries, "O, I prithee no more, I am full of her," and the reader gives him quick sympathy. Cupid next describes Philautia, and after the ladies have exchanged a few more words he unweariedly starts to describe Phantaste, but Mercury has had enough, and breaks in with "Her very name speaks her, let her pass."
>
> Pages pass across the stage to get water from the Fountain of Self Love, and the act closes.

No comment is needed.

---

[1] Cf. Supra, pp. 31-33.

The Poetaster.

ARGUMENT.—The scene is laid in Rome in the time of Augustus. The poet Ovid, despite the reproaches of his father, neglects the study of the law and spends his time writing verses in the company of his mistress, Julia, daughter of Augustus. His companions are Gallus and Tibullus, with their mistresses. They assemble at the house of Albius, a citizen, whose pretty wife, Chloe, longs to join in court life, and is instructed in it by Cytheris, Gallus' mistress. To the company are added Captain Tucca, a whimsical, bragging rascal who lives on his friends, and Crispinus, the "Poetaster," who writes bad verses and hates Horace for his talent and position. Chloe is deeply impressed by Tucca and also by Crispinus, both of whom pay her attentions by which her husband Albius considers himself honored.

The company are invited by Julia to a court banquet, at which the guests impersonate the several gods, Ovid being Jupiter, and Julia, Juno. In the midst the revels are interrupted by the entrance of Cæsar and Horace who have been informed of the event by the tribune, Lupus. Cæsar, enraged at discovering his daughter in such company, orders her imprisonment and Ovid's banishment. The others are pardoned.

Crispinus and Tucca, in retaliation for what they choose to consider Horace's malice, accuse him of treason, and the credulous tribune Lupus arrests him and Mecaenas. They easily clear themselves, and Cæsar punishes their accusers. A counter-accusation is then brought against Crispinus and another writer, Demetrius, for libelling Horace in a play. They are convicted and Horace administers to Crispinus some pills to purge him of the impossible words he uses in his writing. He vomits these words up in succession and is then directed to maintain a careful diet, eschewing all but classic authors.

In the course of the play episodic scenes are inserted to satirize the characters of Crispinus, Demetrius and Tucca, and to magnify the virtues of Horace.

The act-structure is in no way significant, nor is the play as a whole, except as a personal satire on men of Jonson's time. Undoubtedly most of the characters if not all were meant to stand for real persons. Horace is Jonson, Crispinus is Marston, Demetrius is Dekker. The rest are less certain.[1] Being thus deliberately planned

---

[1] For a full discussion of this question, cf. J. H. Penniman's *The War of the Theatres*.

for purposes of personal invective, the play has little dramatic interest. Jonson seems scarcely to have tried to put it into good form.

EPICOENE, OR THE SILENT WOMAN.

ARGUMENT.—Morose, a rich old man, has an abhorrance of any noise except the sound of his own voice. Some practical jokes have been played on him by the young people who know him, and he attributes them all to his nephew and heir, Dauphine. Accordingly he disinherits him, and plans to marry that he may have a son of his own to come into his wealth. Hearing of a woman of so few words that she is dubbed "the Silent Woman," he has her brought to him and marries her.

Dauphine and two friends, Clerimont and Truewit, have been invited by a silly dandy, La-Foole, to a banquet which he means to hold at the house of his kinswoman, Mistress Otter. The other guests are the "collegiate ladies," Haughty, Centaure, and Mavis, with Sir John Daw, and Captain Otter. Dauphine, Clerimont and Truewit, learning of Morose's marriage, persuade the company to transfer their banquet to Morose's house. The change is made, and the company invades the bridegroom's house. The bride now proves as talkative as the other ladies, the banqueters indulge in noisy revelry and Morose flees in consternation to the remotest nook in his house.

After the discovery that his wife can talk, Morose tries to get a divorce. The three young men send him two accomplices, disguised as a clergyman and a lawyer, to advise him, but no remedy seems available. As he is in despair, Dauphine promises to relieve him of his noisy spouse if he in turn will give up part of his income, and guarantee the entire inheritance to his nephew. Morose agrees, and Dauphine then removes the Silent Woman's disguise, and shows her to be really a boy, whom Dauphine had trained to act this part.

An elaborate episode is the joke played by the young men upon Daw and La-Foole. Both are cowards, and each is persuaded that the other is seeking his life. In the presence of the ladies, Daw allows himself to be kicked by Dauphine, whose face is muffled so that he passes for La-Foole. La-Foole is then blind-folded and similarly abused by Dauphine, whom he takes to be Daw. Other tricks are played on these two "gulls" and others of the party.

The play is a farcical embodiment of the typical Jonsonian comedy. Its action has, however, more unity than many of the plays. It has fewer characters, and the episodes are carefully subordinated to the main action, which is the trick on Morose. There is the usual division into dupers and duped, Morose being the chief victim, La-Foole and Daw subordinate ones, while the three friends aim a running fire of ridicule at the rest of the company, especially at the "collegiate ladies" who are counterparts of the French *preciuses*.

BARTHOLOMEW FAIR.

ARGUMENT.—Mistress Littlewit and her husband are anxious to see the sights of Bartholomew Fair. They manage to overcome the religious scruples of Mrs. Littlewit's Puritan mother, Dame Purecraft, and of her spiritual adviser, Zeal-of-the-land Busy, and all four go to eat roast pig at the Fair.

To the Fair also comes Bartholomew Cokes, a half-witted wealthy youth, with his man Waspe, and Grace Wellborn, whom he is to marry. She is averse to the match, but her guardian, Justice Overdo, is Cokes' brother-in-law, and compels the marriage to keep Grace's wealth in the family. In the confusion of the Fair, Cokes loses the rest of his party; he gets his pocket picked, his hat, cloak and sword are stolen, and he turns up at the end of the play like a plucked chicken.

Two young men, Quarlous and Winwife, have been wooing Dame Purecraft, but now fall in love with Grace, who is willing to marry any intelligent and respectable man rather than the fool Cokes. She chooses by lot, and Winwife is designated. Quarlous then resumes his attentions to Dame Purecraft, and succeeds in getting her promise.

Justice Overdo comes to the Fair in disguise, in order the better to ferret out roguery and be able to punish it. He however misunderstands what he sees, mistakes vice for virtue, and in the course of his meddling gets beaten and put in the stocks.

Zeal-of-the-land Busy also meets the same fate as punishment for his denunciation of the heathen follies of the Fair.

Winwife, by a trick, succeeds in getting Justice Overdo's signature to a marriage license for himself and Grace.

All the important persons finally assemble at a puppet-show, where a play written by Littlewit is presented. Zeal-of-the-land Busy breaks in to remonstrate against all stage plays, but is worsted in argument. Justice Overdo then throws off his disguise, and begins to make accusations based on his observations during the day, but is shamed into silence by the discovery of his wife in a rather disgraceful situation. He gives over his attempt at justice, and invites all the company to his house to supper.

It would be useless to give an account of all the incidents which occur as episodes in the play. The argument as stated indicates the general scheme, and the character of the comic action. The victim-in-chief is Bartholomew Cokes. He sums up his adventures fairly comprehensively when in the fourth act he says plaintively:

"Do but carry me home. . . . . I have lost myself, and my cloke, and my hat, and my fine sword, and my sister, and Numps, [i. e. his man, Humphrey Waspe], and mistress Grace, a gentlewoman that I should have married, and a cut-work handkerchief she gave me, and two purses, to-day; and my bargain of hobby-horses and gingerbread, which grieves me worst of all."[1]

Other victims are, Justice Overdo, Waspe, and Zeal-of-the-land Busy. The rest are less important. The chief intriguers are Edgworth, a pick-pocket; Nightengale, a ballad-singer in league with him; Quarlous and Winwife. The rest of the characters are sometimes duped themselves, sometimes dupers of others.

The plan of the play allows the widest license in the treatment, which has a character of spontaneity and freedom from pharisaism rather rare in Jonson. The quality of the comic is coarse but, on the whole, healthy. If we except *The Case Is Altered*, the laughter in this play is the most good-natured Jonson ever indulged in.

---

[1] Act IV, Sc. 2; Works, IV, 448.

The Devil is An Ass.

ARGUMENT.—Pug, a devil, begs Satan to let him visit earth. Satan warns him that he cannot cope with the wickedness of mortals, but allows him to try his luck for a single day. Pug enters the body of a criminal, just hung, steals some clothes, and engages himself as a servant to Fitzdottrel, a gentleman. Fitzdottrel has been imposed upon by Meercraft, a "projector," i. e. one who offers elaborate plans for making men suddenly rich. He has promised Fitzdottrel to recover the "drowned lands" of England for him, and make him "Duke of Drown'd-land," and meanwhile he gets money out of the future duke. Meercraft in his turn has to divide his gains with a thriftless cousin named Everill, who threatens blackmail if money is refused.

Fitzdottrel has a pretty wife, with whom a young man, Wittipol, is in love. To get a glimpse of her, Wittipol offers Fitzdottrel a costly cloak, on condition of being allowed to talk to his wife, in his presence for a quarter of an hour. Fitzdottrel agrees, and during the quarter hour Wittipol openly makes love to Mrs. Fitzdottrel and tells her what a fool her husband is.

After the interview, Wittipol discovers that his friend Manly's apartments are opposite Mrs. Fitzdottrel's across a narrow street. He succeeds in procuring an interview with the lady, but they are discovered by her husband, who challenges Wittipol. Fitzdottrel had been informed of the interview by his servant Pug, who had previously made love to Mrs. Fitzdottrel and been repulsed.

Fitzdottrel, expecting to be shortly made duke, fears that his wife may not comport herself as befits his new dignity and Meercraft suggests that she be sent to a Spanish Lady, who gives instruction in manners. Fitzdottrel agrees, and sends by Pug a valuable ring to the Spanish Lady, with a request that she receive his wife. This lady is a figment of Meercaft's, and the impostor now casts about for some one to act the part and share with him the profits of the office. Wittipol agrees to act, for the sake of seeing Mrs. Fitzdottrel. He disguises himself as a lady, and meets Mr. and Mrs Fitzdottrel. Fitzdottrel is deeply impressed by the Spanish Lady, and after committing his wife to her care proceeds to make over to her temporarily his estate also, as a preliminary to pursuing his quarrel with Wittipol. Meercraft whispers to the lady that this will not be valid, and suggests that his own name be used instead. Wittipol, however, (as the Spanish Lady) wisely bids Fitzdottrel make Manly the feoffee. and this is done.

Wittipol meanwhile has revealed to Mrs. Fitzdottrel his identity, and offered her his devotion. She begs him to be her true friend, not her lover, and to help her against the follies of her husband. He reponds to the appeal, and after the deed of feoffment is drawn, throws off his disguise and tells Fitzdottrel that he is a fool, and his wife is too good for him. Moreover, he refuses to give up the deed of the estates.

Fitzdottrel, by the advice of Meercraft and Everill, now pretends to be possessed of a devil, and accuses his wife of witchcraft, thus hoping to prove that the deed of the estates was invalid. In his ravings he accuses Wittipol and Manly as well, and quite convinces Justice Eitherside, who is called in to hear the testimony.

Meantime, Pug has been arrested by the man from whom he stole his clothes, and sent to Newgate, whence he is rescued by Satan, who carries him off back to Hell. An explosion accompanies this event, and the wardens entering find only the dead body of the thief, and clouds of brimstone fumes. News of the event reaches Justice Eitherside as Fitzdottrel is in his raving The realization that he has had a real devil for servant startles him out of his part, and he confesses the hoax. Manly and Wittipol in turn testify to the blameless character of his wife.

The play has the characters and the turn of plot familiar to readers of Jonson. There is the comic butt Pug, to take general abuse and occasional beatings; there is the familiar impostor, Meercraft, and his chief dupe, Fitzdottrel, with less important victims who have been passed over in giving the argument; there are the young men, Manly and Wittipol, who always control events for their own purposes. Thus in its general nature the play shows nothing new, while in its detailed working out it is full of reminders of earlier work: Meercraft has traits like Sir Politick in *Volpone* and like Subtle in *The Alchemist;* the ladies who talk with the Spanish Lady make us think of the collegiates in *Epicoene*, though the treatment here is by no means so masterly; indeed, the whole plan of the scene where Wittipol plays the rôle of lady is similar to the scenes in the earlier play where the Silent Woman plays her part. There is, however, in this play no clear line of action as is the case where Jonson is at his best. The author appears to be trying to do too many things at once. He does not seem able to manage all his characters, and the play has too many loose ends, so that it lacks the merits of either spontaneity on the one hand or careful finish on the other.

THE STAPLE OF NEWS.

ARGUMENT.—Pennyboy Junior, a youth just of age, has by his father's sudden death come into his inheritance. The first to inform him of his father's death was an old beggar, or "canter," whom out of gratitude the joyful heir keeps with him. Picklock, his father's lawyer, informs the youth that he was by his father destined, to marry the Lady Pecunia, Infanta of the mines, who is now in the care of his uncle, Pennyboy Senior. Pennyboy Jr., therefore, visits her and is well received.

There has just been established an office, called the Staple of News, which claims to issue none but the most reliable news, collected from all over the world. The heir visits the office and takes Pecunia to see it. The officials crowd about her, and Cymbal, master of the office, woos her, hoping to secure her favor for their enterprise.

In honor of his lady, Pennyboy Jr. invites them all to dinner at the Apollo. Here he sets on the rest to compliment his lady, and in his delight at each new compliment makes her kiss the author of it. The merriment rises, and when Pennyboy Sr. breaks in and tries to get the lady and her attendants to return to his house, they flatly refuse, and he is kicked out by the young men.

In the midst of the feast, however, the supposed beggar throws off his rags and reveals himself as the father of the heir. He tells the astonished company that he had his death given out that he might see how his son would manage riches. He ends by reproaching the youth for his prodigality and for his foolishness in making his lady's favors common property, and tells the boy that having abused wealth he shall try beggary for a while.

Picklock, however, hopes to gain something for himself out of the complication. He had been in the secret, and had held in trust the deed of the Pennyboy property, and he now approaches the young heir with the proposal that they retain these papers and compel the father to yield. The father comes in and demands them, but Picklock now declares that they were left him not in trust but in absolute gift. Pennyboy Jr., however, now sides with his father, he reveals Picklock's recent proposal which had involved an admission of the trust, and produces a witness who had heard the conversation from a place of concealment. Picklock, moreover, learns that the deeds have accidentally been delivered to the wrong party and finds himself thus completely foiled.

This brings about a reconciliation between father and son, and they go with Pecunia to visit Pennyboy Sr., who has gone mad because of the desertion of his niece. They find him keeping a law court, with his two dogs as criminals. The return of Pecunia restores him to his reason, and he promises to abandon his miserly ways. He gives over the lady, as well as all his possessions, to Pennyboy Junior.

As has already been pointed out,[1] the most interesting thing in this play is its use of allegory in the passages where the Lady Pecunia appears. Thus the usurer, Pennyboy Senior, says to her:

"All this nether world
Is yours, you command it, and do sway it;
The honor of it, and the honesty,
The reputation, ay, and the religion,
(I was about to say, and had not err'd,)
Is queen Pecunia's : for that style is yours,
If mortals knew your grace, or their own good.[2]

The point of the play is certainly the moral it enforces as to the proper use of wealth, but the reader's mind is somewhat confused by the fact that the play is only partly allegorical. Pennyboy Junior has real wealth, which he inherits, and with which he pays his tailor and his hatter; but he also has this symbolic or figurative wealth in the person of the lady Pecunia. He spends his real gold lavishly, and he is also prodigal in bestowing on others his lady's favors. His uncle, on the other hand, has the opposite vice of miserliness. Pecunia and her maids thus accuse him:

Pecunia. "Never unfortunate princess
Was used so by a jailor. Ask my women:
Band, you can tell, and Statute, how he has used me,
Kept me close prisoner, under twenty bolts——

---

[1] Cf. supra, pp. 36, 37.
[2] *The Staple of News,* Act II, Sc. 1; Works V, 190, 191.

>   *Statute.* And forty padlocks ——
>   *Band.* All malicious engines
>   A wicked smith could forge out of his iron;
>   As locks and keys, shackles and manacles,
>   To torture a great lady. . . . .
>   * * * * * * * * * * *
>   *Pecunia.* But once he would have smother'd me in a
>   chest.
>   And strangled me in leather, but that you
>   Came to my rescue then, and gave me air.
>   *Statute.* For which he cramm'd us up in a close box,
>   All three together, where we saw no sun
>   In one six months.[1]

Finally, Pecunia herself thus exhorts the spectators:

> "And so Pecunia herself doth wish,
> That she may still be aid unto their uses,
> Not slave unto their pleasures, or a tyrant
> Over their fair desires; but teach them all
> The golden mean; the prodigal how to live;
> The sordid and the covetous how to die:
> That, with sound mind; this, safe frugality."[2]

There is nothing further of interest in the structure of the play. Its treatment of allegory, however, might reward special investigation, especially when considered in connection with the quasi-allegorical work of other satirists.

THE MAGNETIC LADY.

ARGUMENT.—Sir Moth Interest, an unscrupulous usurer, has for many years had the keeping of his niece Placentia's dowry, which at her mother's death was given into his charge to be paid down when the girl should make such a marriage as met the approval of her aunt, Lady Loadstone. Placentia has several suitors, and all gather at Lady Loadstone's house. Compass, a friend of Lady Loadstone,

---

[1] Works, V, 260, 261.
[2] Ib., 291.

plans a dinner to be held there, and persuades his brother, Captain Ironside, to join them. At the dinner Ironside gets into a quarrel with Sir Diaphanous Silkworm, an elegant courtier, one of the suitors for Placentia's hand. The captain grows violent and the guests are terrified, especially Placentia, who is carried swooning to her room. The doctor is summoned, and it is presently rumored that the young girl has given birth to a child. The news reaches Sir Diaphanous and the captain just as they are about to fight a duel. They are instantly reconciled, for Sir Diaphanous considers himself indebted to the captain, since his violence was the indirect means of exposing the character of the lady Sir Diaphanous had hoped to marry. The knight promptly retracts his offers of marriage, as do the other suitors.

Compass meanwhile chances to overhear a conversation between Placentia's nurse and Mistress Polish, an attendant of Lady Loadstone's, by which he learns that Placentia is really Polish's daughter, while Pleasance, Placentia's maid, who has been passed off by Polish as her own child, is really the heiress. Compass has long loved Pleasance, and acting on his new knowledge he secretly marries her.

Sir Moth Interest is rejoiced at the news regarding Placentia, as it releases him from any obligation to pay the dowry. But through the efforts of Polish and the nurses the rumor is denied. One of the suitors, Bias, to whom Sir Moth has lent money, now agrees to marry Placentia and to be satisfied with the payment of the original dowry, without interest, and minus a certain amount which Sir Moth has lent him. On these terms Sir Moth pushes the marriage, and announces it to the assembled household. Compass, however, produces his evidence that Pleasance is the heiress, and Sir Moth is finally obliged to pay the dowry with interest. The rumor concerning Placentia now proves well-founded, and Bias withdraws from the contract, and Placentia is left to marry the steward, Needle, father of her child. Lady Loadstone offers herself in marriage to Captain Ironside.

The plot of the play is, in the prominence given to the serious plot, and in the character of this plot, a little like some of the Roman comedies. The supposedly comic situations are found in the discomfiture of the various victims.

The traces of allegory in the treatment of Lady Loadstone and Captain Ironside have been already noted.[1]

---

[1] Cf. Supra, p. 37.

It is hard to see why Jonson chose to insert them, for their "magnetic" qualities have nothing to do with the play.

THE NEW INN.

ARGUMENT.—Lord and Lady Frampul had two daughters. Lady Frampul, downcast by her husband's grief at having no sons, left her home and was not heard of again. The younger daughter also disappeared. Lord Frampul, filled with remorse, set out in search of his wife, but for long years failed to find her. In their absence, the remaining daughter, assuming the title of Lady Frampul, ruled the estate. Here the play opens.

Lord Lovell, melancholy through love of Lady Frampul, is lodged at the New Inn. There arrive at the inn Lady Frampul herself, with her maid, Prudence, and two of her followers, Lords Latimer and Beaufort. The lady has purposed to have a day of merriment and has appointed Prue queen of the revels. Prue invites Lord Lovell to join the party, and after some hesitation he consents.

Lady Frampul being alone with so many gentlemen, Prue plans to give her support by dressing up the host's son, Frank, as a lady. This is done and he is introduced to the company as Lady Frampul's kinswoman, Letitia. Lord Beaufort instantly falls in love with her. Prue now decrees that Lord Lovell shall spend two hours of the day in speaking before Lady Frampul the praises of love, his reward to be a kiss for each hour. The court being set, Lord Lovell fulfills his first hour, praising love to such good effect that the Lady becomes really in love with him.

At this moment a new lady is announced, who, on being brought up, proves to be the wife of Lady Frampul's tailor, dressed, moreover, in the very gown which had been specially ordered for Prudence for this day. The woman is stripped of the gown and sent home in disgrace.

The second hour now comes, in which Lovell, at Lady Frampul's request, changes his theme from love to valor. At the end the second kiss is given, and then, Prue forbidding all further mention of love, Lovell goes disconsolate to bed.

At this moment it is learned that Lord Beaufort has married the lady he has been so industriously courting. As the newly-made couple enter, the host pulls off the lady's disguise and exhibits his son, Frank. But in the midst of the laugh that follows, Frank's old nurse enters, crying distractedly that her daughter is ruined, married to a stranger. It is now discovered that Frank is really a girl after all, who had been brought as a child to the host, and sold to him by the old nurse. Beaufort now refuses to hold to the marriage with a foundling; whereupon the nurse announces that the child is no other than Letitia, younger sister of Lady Frampul, while the nurse is really her mother, the elder Lady Frampul. At this the Host reveals himself as Lord Frampul, and the family are thus reunited. Lord Frampul gives his younger daughter to Beaufort, the elder one to Lord Lovell, while Prue is married to Lord Latimer.

There are a number of interspersed scenes in which the servants of the house figure. The comedy of these scenes is purely episodic and very poor.

The setting of this play has a romantic cast, and with different treatment the play might have been made a "romantic" comedy. As it stands it can scarcely be called such; too much bulk is devoted to the low comedy of the servant scenes and to the incident of the tailor's wife, while the other parts have not the right touch; the treatment is a surface one without being delicate or light. The discourses on love and honor are disproportionately long, and the work as a whole is heavy. Yet it is quite diverse from Jonson's typical manner. There is in the main action no attempt at satire, there are no intriguers and no victims, and the resolution is a result of chance, whose end is to make marriages, not to expose folly and vice. On the whole, then, the play is nearer the romantic than the satiro-comic type, but when contrasted with *The Case Is Altered*, it shows that Jonson's hand had lost the cunning of earlier years.

THE CASE IS ALTERED.

ARGUMENT.—Count Ferneze, of Milan, has one son, Paolo, another having been lost in infancy. Paolo, about to depart with the Milanese General, Maximilian, to fight against the French, confesses to his friend Angelo that he loves a poor girl, Rachel, daughter of Jaques, a Jew, who is apparently poor, but who really possesses a hoard of gold. Angelo promises to be her protector. He himself, however, falls in love with her, as do also Ferneze, his steward Christophero, and Onion, a groom of the palace. Christophero and Ferneze both ask Jaques for Rachel in marriage, which throws him into violent perturbation lest they suspect his riches. Ferneze, hearing that Paolo is taken prisoner, is recalled to paternal duty and relinquishes the pursuit of Rachel.

Maximilian returns from battle, bringing as prisoners Lord Chamont and Gasper, his servant. Ferneze proposes to exchange them for his son, and sends the servant to arrange the affair. In reality, however, it is Lord Chamont whom he sends, for the prisoners had changed names. When it is too late, Ferneze discovers the cheat, and in his rage threatens to kill Gasper.

Meanwhile Angelo plots to get possession of Rachel. He pretends to be helping Christophero in his suit, and shows him how to lure Jaques away from the house. Angelo promises to steal Rachel while Jaques is away, and bring her to Christophero. To Rachel he says that Paolo is returning and wishes to meet her. On this understanding Rachel accompanies him, but she soon discovers that Angelo's real purpose is to get her in his power.

At this juncture Paolo, who has just been exchanged, really appears and rescues Rachel. Angelo, overcome with contrition, is forgiven for his treachery.

Maximilian, thinking that his son will not return, is about to kill Gasper, when Paolo arrives with Chamont. It is then discovered that Gasper is really Ferneze's other son, thought dead, and that Rachel is a long lost sister of Chamont. Chamont marries one of Ferneze's daughters. Paolo marries Rachel.

The plot is, of course, derived from the *Aulularia* and the *Captivi* of Plautus. For a discussion of it, see chapter V.

A Tale of a Tub.

ARGUMENT.—Young Squire Tub, of Totten Court, is in love with Audrey Turfe, whose father is constable in a neighboring village. Early in the morning of Valentine's day Canon Hugh arrives at Totten Court and warns the squire that Audrey is about to be married to a villager, John Clay. They arrange a plan of interfering with the wedding, and Tub fees the canon for his help.

Sir Hugh then posts off to Justice Preamble, who is also in love with Audrey, and informs him that the girl is to be married, but that Squire Tub is planning to get possession of her. He suggests to the Justice a way of circumventing Tub, and gets from Preamble another fee for his intelligence.

Meanwhile, Lady Tub, the Squire's mother, missing her son, sends her servant, Martin, to hunt for him, and she herself also sets out with her maid.

As the wedding party is ready to go to church, it is broken up by the entrance of Hilts, Squire Tub's servant, dressed as if for a long journey. He announces that his master, one Captain Thums, has been attacked and robbed, and appeals to Constable Turfe to "raise the hue and cry" after the robbers. Of one of the robbers Hilts gives a description that fits John Clay, and Turfe thereupon finds himself bound to arrest his son-in-law elect. Clay however, runs away and hides.

In the confusion Squire Tub comes in and carries off Audrey, but is met by Preamble with his servant, Metaphor, in a borrowed pursuivant's coat. Metaphor places Tub under arrest and Preamble goes off with Audrey, but at this moment Hilts reënters, and frightens Metaphor into confessing that the whole is a plot of Preamble's to get Audrey. Tub immediately seeks out Turfe and tells him that the whole affair of the "hue and cry" was an invention of Preamble's and that Preamble is about to marry his daughter. Turfe promptly pursues the pair, stops the marriage, and brings Audrey home again.

Preamble and Hugh make another plot. Hugh, in disguise, goes to Turfe's house, presents himself as Captain Thums and accuses the constable of negligence in not finding the robbers. He carries the bewildered constable off to Preamble's house and the two conspirators persuade Turfe that in default of producing Clay he must give Captain Thums a hundred pounds. Turfe authorizes Metaphor to fetch the money from home, and they add a whispered direction to him to bring Audrey as well.

Metaphor, however, as he is returning, again falls in with Hilts and Tub, who by mingled threats and bribes persuade him to leave the money and the girl with them. At this moment however, Lady Tub enters, her suspicions are aroused at seeing her son with Audrey, and she summons him to go with her, while Audrey she entrusts to Martin to be taken home.

The squire finally gets free of his mother, finds Martin and bids him dress out Audrey in Lady Tub's clothes and bring her thus disguised to Totten court, where the squire will marry her. He also invites Turfe and the other villagers to the house to see a masque.

All assemble, among them Martin, bringing in Audrey, dressed like a fine lady. It is then discovered that Martin has outwitted the squire, Preamble and old Turfe, by marrying Audrey himself, and that Cannon Hugh performed the ceremony without recognizing Audrey. The other suitors, however, accept the inevitable, and the play ends with a masque, presented by two of the villagers, in which are set forth the day's adventures.

The play, taken by Gifford for a work of the poet's old age, is now thought to have been one of his first efforts.[1] The character of the play itself would seem to bear this out, for there is no humor-study of the typical Jonsonian sort. Yet, on the other hand, the useless allegorical touches in the treatment of metaphor are more like his later than his earlier work. There is little effort made to mark off the characters vividly, though the talk of the villagers, which is in dialect, gives a realistic touch. The source of the comic effects is in surprising incident, not in character contrast. Canon Hugh sets the plot going, and the first act presents the four elements of the action: (1) Turfe, with his plan to marry Audrey to Clay; (2) Squire Tub, planning to trick Turfe and marry Audrey; (3) Justice Preamble, planning to circumvent Tub, and marry Audrey; (4) Lady Tub, bent on keeping her son from marrying. Audrey is passed about from hand to hand till Martin steps in and resolves the plot by marrying her himself. There is little satire in the play except the masque scenes, which ridicule Inigo Jones, and which were probably later interpolations. The play has, therefore, not the form of a satiric comedy: there is no distinct group of intriguers who successfully lay traps for the victims. There is, indeed, plenty of scheming and trickery, nearly every one is trying to trick some one else, but nearly every one gets tricked in turn, and at the end no one can laugh at his fellow or claim superiority, unless it be Martin, who by a lucky chance has won the prize.

---

[1] Cf. Cunningham's note, Works, I, pp. xiii-xvii.

BIBLIOGRAPHY.

Amiel, H. F.: Journal. London, 1889.
Aristotle: Poetics. Ed. S. H. Butcher. London, 1895.
Aronstein, Philipp: Ben Jonson's Theorie des Lustspiels. Anglia, XVII (neue folge, V.)
Brink, Bernhard ten: Five Lectures on Shakespeare, translated by Julia Franklin. New York, 1895.
Buff, A.: The Quarto Edition of 'Every Man in His Humour.' Englische Studien, I.
Coleridge, S. T.: Literary Remains. Ed. H. N. Coleridge. London, 1836.
Congreve, William: Comedies. Ed. W. E. Henley. Chicago and London, 1895.
Corbin, John: The Elizabethan Hamlet. London and New York, 1895.
Corneille, Pierre: Oeuvres. Ed. Mary-Laveaux. Paris, 1862.
Dowden, Edward: Shakspere: A Critical Study of His Mind and Art. London, 1875.
Everett, C. C.: Poetry, Comedy and Duty. New York, 1890.
Fleay, F. G.: A Biographical Chronicle of the English Drama. London, 1891.
Freytag, Gustav: The Technique of the Drama, translated by E. J. MacEwan. Chicago, 1895.
Friesen, H. Freiherr von: Ben Jonson. Eine Studie. Elze's Jahrbuch der Deutschen Shakespeare-Gesellschaft, X.
Haslewood, Joseph: The Arte of English Poesie. London, 1815.
Hazlitt, William: Lectures on the English Comic Writers. Edited by his son. London, 1841.

Holthausen, F.: Die Quelle von Ben Jonson's Volpone. Anglia, XII.
Jonson Ben: Works, with notes and a biographical memoir by W. Gifford, with introduction and appendices, by F. Cunningham. London, 1875.
——Timber; or Discoveries. Ed. F. E. Shelling. Boston, 1892.
——Best Plays. Ed. Brinsley Nicholson, with an introduction by C. H. Herford. London, 1893-94.
Koeppel, Emil: Quellen-Studien zu den Dramen Ben Jonson's, John Marston's und Beaumont's und Fletcher's. Erlangen and Leipzig, 1893.
Lamb, Charles: Dramatic Essays. Ed. Brander Matthews. New York, 1891.
——Specimens of the English Dramatic Poets. London, 1890.
Longinus: On the Sublime. Translated by H. L. Havell, with an introduction by Andrew Lang. London, 1890.
Meredith, George: An Essay on Comedy, and the Uses of the Comic Spirit. New York, 1897.
Molière: Oeuvres. Ed. Eugene Despois. Paris, 1876.
Moulton, R. G: The Ancient Classical Drama. Oxford, 1890.
Paget, Violet (Vernon Lee): Studies of the Eighteenth Century in Italy. London, 1887.
Penniman, Josiah H.: The War of the Theatres. Boston, 1897.
Puttenham, George: The Art of English Poesie. In Haslewood's Ancient Critical Essays. London, 1811.
Reinhardstoettner, Carl: Spätere Bearbeitungen Plautinischer Lustspiele. Leipzig, 1886.
Saegelken, Heinrich: Ben Jonson's Römer-Dramen. Bremen, 1880.

Schmidt, I.: Ueber Ben Jonson's Maskenspiele.
Schopenhauer, Arthur: The World as Will and Idea. Translated by R. B. Haldane and John Kemp. London, 1886.
Sidney, Sir Philip: Defense of Poesy. Ed. Albert S. Cook. Boston, 1890.
Swinburne, A. C.: A Study of Ben Jonson. London, 1889.
Symonds, J. A.: Ben Jonson. New York, 1886.
Votke, Th.: Ben Jonson in seinen Anfängen. Herrig's Archive, Band 71.
Wilke, W.: Anwendung der Rhyme-test und Double-endings-test auf Ben Jonson's Dramen. Anglia, X.
Wylie, L. J.: Studies in the Evolution of English Criticism. Boston, 1884.

INDEX.

Aristophanes, 8, 21, 22, 25, 26, 27, 33.
Aristotle, 11, 14, 15, 16, 19.
Bacon, 13, 14, 32.
Browning, 38.
Coleridge, 36.
Congreve, 14, 27, 34.
Corneille, 16, 19.
Cowley, 12.
Dekker, 84.
Dion Cassius, 20.
Donne, 6.
Dowden, 17.
Dryden, 6, 11, 12, 14, 19, 20.
Freytag, 37.
Gifford, 36, 82.
Gilbert, 25.
Hazlitt, 35.
Hegel, 38.
Horace, 14.
James, Henry, 22.
Jones, Inigo, 98.
Jonson, *Alchemist*, 6, 16, 29, 31, 36, 37, 38, 46, 55, 60-4, 66, 67, 68, 69, 71, 89; *Bartholomew Fair*, 29, 30, 31, 37, 38, 86-7; *Case Is Altered*, 16 (note), 73-79, 87, 95-6; *Catiline*, 12, 17, 31, 72; *Cynthia's Revels*, 29, 30, 31, 32 (note), 33, 75, 82-83; *Devil Is an Ass*, 88-90 *Epicoene*, 30, 31, 33, 36, 85-86, 89; *Every Man in His Humour*, 17 (note), 29, 46-55, 64, 73; *Every Man Out of His Humour*, 6, 29, 31, 32 (and note), 35, 46, 49, 55-60; *Magnetic Lady*, 37, 92-4; *New Inn*, 94-5; *Poetaster*, 7, 29, 30, 31, 33, 84-5; *Sad Shepherd*, 79; *Sejanus*, 12, 17, 18, 19, 30, 31, 32, 66, 71, 72; *Staple of News*, 37, 90-2; *Tale of a Tub*, 96-8; *Volpone*, 6, 29, 30, 31, 32, 33, 36, 37, 38, 46, 55, 64-72, 89.
Juvenal, 8, 27.
Longinus, 9 (note), 10, 11.

Lyly, 12.
Marston, 84.
Massinger, 44, 45, 54.
Menander, 26, 27, 33.
Meredith, 25.
Middlemarch, 38.
Middleton, 44, 54.
Milton, 7, 8, 14.
Molière, 8, 17, 21, 25, 27, 31, 34, 37, 38, 75; *Tartuffe*, 38, 68; *Le Misanthrope*, 68, 69.
Moulton, 31, 83.
Munday, Anthony, 74.
Pater, 13.
Plautus, 49, 53, 73, 78, 96.
Puttenham, 5.
Schelling, E., 12.
Schopenhauer, 17.
Seneca, 19, 73.
Shakespeare, 5, 8, 18, 21, 22, 25, 27, 32, 39, 40, 41, 43, 54, 73, 78; *All's Well that Ends Well*, 74; *As You Like It*, 40, (Rosalind and Celia), 77; *Comedy of Errors*, 24, 73, 75; *Hamlet*, 48, 49; *King Henry IV*, 26, (Falstaff) 23, 24, 26; *King Lear*, 21; *Love's Labour's Lost*, 73, 74, 75; *Merchant of Venice*, 73; *Merry Wives of Windsor*, 26; *Midsummer Night's Dream*, 40, 73; *Much Ado about Nothing*, 40; *Romeo and Juliet*, 41, 42; *Twelfth Night*, 40; *Two Gentlemen of Verona*, 41, 42, 73, 74-77, (Malvolio) 24, 26, 33.
Sidney, 5, 6, 7, 9, 12, 27.
Sophocles, 14, 18.
Spenser, 5.
Suetonius, 20.
Swift, 27.
Tacitus, 20, 27.
Terence, 26, 27, 43, 44, 45, 53, 54, 73.
Upton, 36.
Whalley, 36.

ERRATA.

Page 10, line 19. *For* we may learn, *etc., read* "We may learn, *etc.*
Page 13, line 27. *For* beautful *read* beautiful.
Page 14, line 26. *After* prescribe *insert a period.*
Page 16, line 32. *Delete the quotation marks.*
Page 23, line 17. *After* man *insert a comma.*
Page 24, line 12. *For* are *read* is.
Page 41, line 3. *For* wished *read* wishes.
Page 42, line 29. *For* severence *read* severance.
Page 43, line 16. *For* are *read* is.
Page 47, line 10. *For* Bobodill *read* Bobadill.
Page 62, line 12. *After* Act *delete the period.*
Page 85, line 5. *For* abhorrance *read* abhorrence.
Page 89, line 1. *For* reponds *read* responds.
Page 94, line 19. *For* the host's son, Frank as a lady *read* the host's son, Frank, as a lady.
Page 98, line 4. *For* Cannon *read* Canon
Page 99, line 16. *For* Mary-Laveaux *read* Marty-Laveaux.
Page 101, line 11. *For* Archive *read* Archiv.

YALE STUDIES IN ENGLISH

ALBERT S. COOK, EDITOR

I. The Foreign Sources of Modern English Versification. Charlton M. Lewis, Ph.D. .50

II. Ælfric: a New Study of his Life and Writings. Caroline Louisa White, Ph.D. . 1.50

III. The Life of St. Cecilia, from MS. Ashmole 43 and MS. Cotton Tiberius E. VII, with Introduction, Variants, and Glossary. Bertha Ellen Lovewell, Ph.D. . . . 1.00

IV. Dryden's Dramatic Theory and Practice. Margaret Sherwood, Ph.D. 50

V. Studies in Jonson's Comedy. Elisabeth Woodbridge, Ph.D. 50

VI. A Guide to the Middle English Metrical Romances dealing with English and Germanic Legends, and with the Cycles of Charlemagne and of Arthur. Anna Hunt Billings, Ph.D. (In preparation) . . 1.50

VII. The Legend of St. Andrew, an Old English Epic, translated into Blank Verse, with an Introduction. Robert Kilburn Root. (In preparation) 50

VIII. Classical Mythology in Milton. Charles Grosvenor Osgood, Jr. (In preparation) .75

LAMSON, WOLFFE AND COMPANY
BOSTON, NEW YORK, AND LONDON

www.ingramcontent.com/pod-product-compliance
Lightning Source LLC
Chambersburg PA
CBHW031419160426
43196CB00008B/991